This book belongs to

_____

_____

_____

_____

# GWEN SHAMBLIN

# Exodus
## Daily Devotional

The Weigh Down Workshop, Inc.®
P.O. Box 689099
Franklin, TN 37068-9099
www.wdworkshop.com
800-844-5208

*EXODUS Daily Devotional,* by Gwen Shamblin

Project Manager: Carole Purkey
Editor: Michelle McDonald
Copy Editors: Lyn Walker, Teresa Stephens, Rob Scobey & Marsha Herndon
Cover & Book Design: Gwen Shamblin
Production: Joe Haubenreich, Bobby Sagmiller & Michelle McDonald

**Published by The Weigh Down Workshop, Inc.®**

The Weigh Down Workshop, Inc.® (and design) is a registered trademark of The Weigh Down Workshop, Inc.®

The Weigh Down Workshop™, Weigh Down™ (and design), WDW™ (and design), Rising Above™ and EXODUS: Out of Egypt™ are trademarks of The Weigh Down Workshop, Inc.®

Scripture taken from the HOLY BIBLE: NEW INTERNATIONAL VERSION®. NIV®. Copyright © 1973, 1978, 1984 by International Bible Society. Used by permission of Zondervan Publishing House.

ISBN 1-892729-00-8
Printed in the United States of America
August 1998
First Edition

# Introduction

We are all travelers on a short journey. On this journey, we find ourselves surrounded by a maze of opportunities with countless choices. The consequences of continually making the wrong choices have led to many a troubling day for most of us. Oh, to wake up and have continual dependence and concentration on God the Father and Jesus Christ the Son!

I pray that the thoughts in this book will help you develop a deeper relationship with God. The Apostle Paul told others to imitate him as he imitated Jesus Christ. He was not being conceited or arrogant, but rather he was desperate to help bring peace into the lives of many seekers. It is, after all, a seeking process—a continual seeking process. Hopefully, this book will help you understand how I think about the Father and how I love Him with all my heart. I believe that the perspective I have about the heart of the heavenly Father has made all the difference in making the choices that I have made over the last few decades.

The God of the universe is trying to get through to us. He is asking us to seek out His personality, His job descriptions, and His governing decisions. He is asking us to love, respect, and trust all the decisions He makes about life and death, love and hate, light and darkness, and yesterday and tomorrow. I cannot express to you how much I love Him and how I love every decision He makes—from the ingenious color of the grass (it could have been purple or brown, but I love green) to the natural process of death to our physical body that brings us home to a new life with Him.

True happiness can be found in an intelligent perspective of what is going on. In John 15:15, Jesus said, "I no longer call you servants, because a servant does not know his master's business. Instead, I have called you friends, for everything that I learned from my Father I have made known to you." The more you learn about the mind of God and experience His plan for your life, the more you can live like a child—full of happiness and peace with excited anticipation about the mystery of each coming day—instead of living each day in worry and fear!

Finally, I hope that the pages of this book will help you understand the wonderful but dangerous jealousy of the Father. We are not to play around with the love of the Father! We should respect and fearfully adore this opportunity to make the right choice to fall in love with Him. It is a daily choice, until the heart is deeply embedded in pure love for the Father.

Hopefully, the scriptures, thoughts, and observations you are about to read will help you develop the above mindset as you learn about His love for you, and as you record your personal journey, expressing where He has directed your heart and mind the day after each new lesson.

With love,

Gwen

# Exodus Basics

# Jesus Is the Cornerstone

*Consequently, you are no longer foreigners and aliens, but fellow citizens with God's people and members of God's household, built on the foundation of the apostles and prophets, with Christ Jesus himself as the chief cornerstone.* —Ephesians 2:19–20

God has brought you here to join the mighty exodus of people who are all moving away from the slavery of food, dieting, bulimia, anorexia and many other strongholds. The miserable state of slavery to food and diets is not unlike the bondage the children of God felt when they were enslaved centuries ago to the Egyptian Pharaohs. The book of Exodus tells us how God's children, once subjugated to Pharaoh, were forced into slave labor to build huge Egyptian structures, such as the pyramids. Those towering icons are representations of the strength and the soul that the Israelites invested in Egypt. May we all reinvest our souls in preparing our hearts to be used to build the church of God with Jesus Christ as the cornerstone.

Start your year out reviewing God's salvation. Review the basics of how God has saved us from having to love this earth and how we get to love Him. What a salvation!

*January 1*

# God, where are You leading me today?

_January 2_

# God Can Deliver You

*During the night Pharaoh summoned Moses and Aaron and said, "Up! Leave my people, you and the Israelites! Go, worship the LORD as you have requested. Take your flocks and herds, as you have said, and go. And also bless me."* ━Exodus 12:31–32

The Exodus story has meaning for us today. This story is foundational and is used throughout the Old Testament and the New Testament and is used for warnings and instruction by Jesus, Stephen, and the Apostle Paul. To start with, I believe that Egypt is symbolic of this earth and anything on earth with which we can fall in love. The symbolism is that we can worship anything and let it then control us—cigarettes, alcohol, money, food, praise of men, etc. Any habit you want to quit, but that now controls you, is what you are bowing down to. What is on your mind and what you find yourself worrying about is your god. But just as God delivered the Israelites from slavery of Pharaoh, He can deliver you today. Make Him your destiny, make Him your one true God, and give Him all the glory. And He will take you away from earthly things and let you go and worship Him instead.

# God, where are You leading me today?

January 4

# A Higher Love

*But the Israelites went through the sea on dry ground, with a wall of water on their right and on their left. That day the LORD saved Israel from the hands of the Egyptians, and Israel saw the Egyptians lying dead on the shore. And when the Israelites saw the great power the LORD displayed against the Egyptians, the people feared the LORD and put their trust in him and in Moses his servant.*        ━Exodus 14:29–31

We have all started off in Egypt. In other words, we have all given our devotion to something on this earth, becoming slaves to the things we love. Since we are slaves to what we love, it will take an even *stronger love* to remove us. God showed the Israelites His passionate, jealous love, and He let them know that He was not going to sit still and let Egypt enslave them. Egypt was exposed for what it was—worthless—and God showed His love and power in an incredible display of devastating plagues and powerful deliverance. The children of God made the right choice and followed Him out of Egypt and into the desert, and finally to the Promised Land. There is no love that compares to the love of God! Follow Him!

# God, where are You leading me today?

January 6

# What Are Your Idols?

*He said to me, "Son of man, have you seen what the elders of the house of Israel are doing in the darkness, each at the shrine of his own idol? They say, 'The LORD does not see us; the LORD has forsaken the land.'" Again, he said, "You will see them doing things that are even more detestable." Then he brought me to the entrance to the north gate of the house of the LORD, and I saw women sitting there, mourning for Tammuz [a false god]. He said to me, "Do you see this, son of man? You will see things that are even more detestable than this."* ━━Ezekiel 8:12–15

Many people have given their love to Egypt and its idols and are not even aware of what they are giving their devotion and energy to. There are several ways to find out if something is an idol in your life. The first is just what we ask people to do in Weigh Down: let the object, such as your extra food, be taken away. If you still long for it, you know that your heart has been given over to that idol. Something even more detestable to God—even more than finding out that you are bowing down to a false god—is seeing you mourning and pining over the idol. If you have tried to separate yourself from food or any stronghold and you are sad about it, this really hurts God.

Another way to identify an idol is to examine what your mind is on all the time. What do you worry about? That is where your heart is. If you find that your heart is enslaved or mourning over an idol, or many idols, pray to the Father to free you from your anguish. Never mourn over the food you have left behind, and strengthen your focus on God each time your heart feels troubled. One day you will realize that God has taken over as your heart's true desire, and you will feel light and free!

# God, where are You leading me today?

January 8

# Are You Hungry and Thirsty for God?

*Blessed are those who hunger and thirst for righteousness, for they will be filled.* —*Matthew 5:6*

God created food to fill our physical bodies, to nourish our muscles and cells, and to give us strength and health. But if you have been in Weigh Down for any time at all, you have realized that mere food is not enough to truly fill our spirits and souls—in fact, it doesn't even come close. That's because that is not the purpose for which food was created. All of us have an inner hunger and thirst for something, and it will not be satisfied by food, money, sexual lust, television, sports, shopping, or any other worldly pursuit. This is a hunger for God, and the only thing that will fill you up is God Himself.

When you recognize this hunger for what it is and you satisfy it with seeking God and His Word and His guidance, you will be righteous in His sight. This is a stronger hunger than any physical hunger, and, likewise, the comfort from His love will satisfy you more than any food could ever satisfy physical hunger. You will be filled!

# God, where are You leading me today?

# The Law of Sin

*Those who live according to the sinful nature have their minds set on what that nature desires; but those who live in accordance with the Spirit have their minds set on what the Spirit desires. The mind of sinful man is death, but the mind controlled by the Spirit is life and peace; the sinful mind is hostile to God. It does not submit to God's law, nor can it do so. Those controlled by the sinful nature cannot please God.* ━━Romans 8: 5–8

The law of sin (overindulgence of any kind, materialism, the love of power or praise, anger, greed or malice, etc.) is somewhat like the law of gravity. It is real, it is strong, it pulls you down, and it is a force that must be reckoned with. If you have never addressed this compelling force of gravity or compelling force of sin head-on, then you might have some bruises when you first begin the process of overcoming. *Strong*holds are well named. You can ignore the law of gravity and come to an early death. In the same way, you can ignore this law of sin (the magnetic pull to the love of worldly things) and come to an early spiritual death. The way to rise above the magnetic pull of sin is to focus off earthly things and onto being happy to do everything God's way because, after all, He is GOD. Practice flying above the pull of all worldly things with a new focus and a new heart. Practice this today, because those controlled by their strongholds *cannot* please God.

*January 11*

# God, where are You leading me today?

January 12

# Temptations and Desire Eating

*When tempted, no one should say, "God is tempting me." For God cannot be tempted by evil, nor does he tempt anyone; but each one is tempted when, by his own evil desire, he is dragged away and enticed. Then, after desire has conceived, it gives birth to sin; and sin, when it is full-grown, gives birth to death.* ━James 1:13–15

Once you begin to wait for true physiological hunger, you discover that there is another feeling of hunger. It is your own "I'm not hungry, but I want it anyway" attitude. We will call this "desire eating" or "head hunger." To help you understand this idea, imagine a headstrong two-year-old child, prone to temper tantrums, who sees a toy, desires it, beats his hands on the floor to speed up the service, then grabs the toy and holds it close with a tightened grip. The desire is very strong, and the temptation to just give in is strong, also. But remember that this temptation does not come from God, but from your own evil desire. Remember, too, that this temptation will lead to sin, which will lead to death. Be aware of your temptations for what they are, and be strong when you stand up to them. Think of God's love for you and run to Him when your temptations are strong, for He is the way to life.

# God, where are You leading me today?

January 14

# Giving Your All to God

*One of the teachers of the law came and heard them debating. Noticing that Jesus had given them a good answer, he asked him, "Of all the commandments, which is the most important?"* ━━Mark 12:28

Jesus answered the above question by telling them that the most important thing is to love God with all of your heart, soul, mind, and strength. Although the journey starts in the mind with knowledge of God, just having the knowledge alone is not enough. You could have the knowledge of God but not love Him at all. We must have a whole heart for God!

We fell in love with food by giving it our heart, soul, mind, and strength, which is all included in the one behavior called obedience. We obeyed the food. It called us from bed in the morning, and we used our strength to prepare it. We also used our strength to force more of it down into the body than the body called for. We gave it our mind all day long by looking through recipe books and discussing the latest diets with our friends, asking, "What do you get to eat on your diet?" We lusted after the foods that were on the menu, and we gave our hearts to the 10 o'clock binge. To convert this love over to God, we need to obey God. Every time we obey God with regard to food or *anything* He puts on our heart to work on, we will fall more in love with Him. We must remember this every day of the year.

*January 15*

# God, where are You leading me today?

# The Crush

*But if from there you seek the LORD your God, you will find him if you look for him with all your heart and with all your soul.* —*Deuteronomy 4:29*

Your first question might be: "What *is* your heart?" Well, the best way to describe loving with your heart is to liken it to the love we have for another person. If you have ever had a crush on someone, then you know how this feels. Your emotions rise and your pulse rate goes up. You know if that person enters the room, for your senses are alert to the voice and presence of the one you love. You think about your heart's love every spare moment. You dress for that person, and you seek out opportunities to be in his or her presence. You look forward to your times alone. Separation brings sadness. You see, your heart is an emotional entity. It has passion and feeling and devotion. God made our hearts, and we all have 100 percent of a heart. However, some people have given pieces of their heart to things in this world that only drain the life out of them until they have no heart left and are burnt out. Seek the Lord as if you had a crush on Him and devote your total heart to Him. Fill your heart's need for passion and devotion by focusing on your loving Father and you *will* find Him.

# God, where are You leading me today?

January 18

# Free from Sin

*What shall we say, then? Shall we go on sinning so that grace may increase? By no means! We died to sin; how can we live in it any longer? Or don't you know that all of us who were baptized into Christ Jesus were baptized into his death? We were therefore buried with him through baptism into death in order that, just as Christ was raised from the dead through the glory of the Father, we too may live a new life. If we have been united with him like this in his death, we will certainly also be united with him in his resurrection. For we know that our old self was crucified with him so that the body of sin might be done away with, that we should no longer be slaves to sin—because anyone who has died has been freed from sin.* —Romans 6: 1–7

One of the strongest statements in the New Testament occurs when the Apostle Paul says that we cannot continue in sin so that grace may abound. "By no means" is a strong statement. You cannot find an argument that will allow you to stay under grace in a blatantly sinning state. Grace will not abound, if that is what you think. Obviously, this was an issue for the early Christians, and Paul sets them straight in the next few chapters of Romans. We should learn from this, too, and realize that since we have died to sin through Jesus, we should *by no means* live in sin any longer.

Sin is simply loving yourself—or anything on this earth or in heaven above—more than God, and sin can be manifested in many ways. The love of God will draw you away from the other loves. By no means will you want to love something more than God as you study His graceful covenant promise to you!

# God, where are You leading me today?

January 20

# God is Better than a Binge

*Taste and see that the LORD is good; blessed is the man who takes refuge in him.*                                                    *—Psalm 34:8*

In the past you may have loved the feeling of planning a binge and dreaming about food. You may have looked forward to the feeling of waiting to be alone so you could prepare, cook, and consume the food without the judgment of anybody. But I'm sure you have learned by now that food cannot satisfy...the world cannot satisfy. This is true if you go after the intoxicated feeling, the antidepressant feeling, the feeling of sexual lust, the tobacco feeling, the love of money feeling, or the love of the praise of people feeling. After you binge on the world and its pleasures, you are empty and are left in need again.

The good news is that you can relearn how to get the satisfied feeling from the Lord. When you feed your longing soul with God, His will, and His personality, and when you experiment with talking to Him, doing things His way, having your prayers answered, and trusting Him, then love for God will fill your heart and the old empty feeling will leave permanently. You start to feel fulfilled—not so "hungry" anymore. You discover that running to God for everything—worries, questions, help, and enjoyment—is delightful and so much better than a binge. Taste and see today!

# God, where are You leading me today?

January 22

# Making the Food Behave

*Since you died with Christ to the basic principles of this world, why, as though you still belonged to it, do you submit to its rules: "Do not handle! Do not taste! Do not touch!"? These are all destined to perish with use, because they are based on human commands and teachings. Such regulations indeed have an appearance of wisdom, with their self-imposed worship, their false humility and their harsh treatment of the body, but they lack any value in restraining sensual indulgence.* —Colossians 2:20–23

There is nothing inherently wrong with food, alcohol, tobacco, credit cards, tranquilizers, and sexual desire. What is wrong is with the *heart*. Making the food have less fat is not going to make our hearts less greedy for food. I'm sure we've all experienced that in the past while on one diet or another. Tearing up a credit card is not going to keep our hearts from materialism. Just ask anyone who has cut up their credit cards only to open new accounts within the year. Locking someone up in a detoxification center to make them stop abusing alcohol or drugs is not going to fix their heart. This is why there are so many people who return to the center once, twice, or many times to repeat the treatment. We can't just change what is around us and expect that to make us behave correctly. Making our food behave by removing the calories, sugar, and fat will not make us desire to eat less—that can only come from the heart. You could change your environment all you want to and yet still be secretly kissing the food. Examine your heart. Where do you truly need to make changes?

# God, where are You leading me today?

_January 24_

# How to Fall in Love

*I love the LORD, for he heard my voice; he heard my cry for mercy. Because he turned his ear to me, I will call on him as long as I live.*

*—Psalm 116:1–2*

We have talked a lot about choosing God. So, what are some more ways to fall in love with God? Think about it. How did you fall in love with food or other strongholds—cigarettes, alcohol, money, or pornography? What happened was that our hearts became enslaved to strongholds by *obeying* the strongholds. Look at food as an example: When the potato chips called our name from the pantry and said, "Hey, come eat me," we found ourselves listening and obeying. When we thought about a great steak dinner, we felt our emotions rise. Our pulse rate went up. Our senses were alert to the sound and presence of popcorn popping, steak sizzling, corn boiling, and candy wrappers opening. We found ourselves dressing for eating occasions, preferring elastic outfits with no belts. We looked forward to times alone for a binge. We would do anything to get to food. Buying, preparing, and eating food was always a pleasure, while being separated from food brought sadness. Now transfer these actions to God. You will be greatly rewarded, for God will hear your cries, whereas the food could not. God will turn His ear to you, whereas the food never could. Transfer your love by listening to, singing to, obeying, dressing for, anticipating, and longing for the Father.

# God, where are You leading me today?

January 26

# The Idolatry of Greed

*Put to death, therefore, whatever belongs to your earthly nature: sexual immorality, impurity, lust, evil desires and greed, which is idolatry.*
*—Colossians 3:5*

The Bible tells us that greed is idolatry, and as strange as that sounds, it is true. Actually, greed is temptation that you feel if you have not experienced God giving you what you think you need when you think you need it. However, once you begin to trust in God's timing and the way He provides for you, you will begin running to Him for everything. When you do this, you will no longer be running to food, and you will not be tempted to take the last ice cream bar before someone else gets to it. You will not run to the restaurant door trying to beat someone to the buffet line. You will not feel your mouth watering for a second helping before you even finished the first. You will not feel that greed for food anymore, because you trust that your God will provide. The idolatry of greed will have been put to death, just as God has instructed!

# God, where are You leading me today?

January 28

# God's Generous Rewards

*And without faith it is impossible to please God, because anyone who comes to him must believe that he exists and that he rewards those who earnestly seek him.* —Hebrews 11:6

We will be giving tips all the way through this book to help you develop a heart that is passionate for the Father. Your first assignment is to take 10 minutes away from food and give it to God. He doesn't need your 10 minutes, so He gives you back 20! Take that 10 dollars away from the drive-through window and give it to God. Our God is *the* God and the *only* God. How do I know? He is the only One who will not only return the money I give Him, but He will also send showers of blessings along with it. He doesn't need your money! However, food will *take* your 10 dollars, as well as your time, and will only ask for more and more. But God has it all, and He generously rewards hearts that love Him. If you run to Him for everything, you will be rewarded with great blessings or jewels.

Running to God for comfort and solutions just makes sense. Do you need a counselor? He knows all truth, and His Word is a light unto your path. Do you need a friend? He is the God of all comfort. Are you low on money, need your roof fixed or your car repaired? God can provide. Are you looking for excitement? His kingdom is dynamic. There is nothing that He cannot do. He is the God that single-handedly defeated Pharaoh and his army and pulled the men, women, children, and livestock out of slavery to worship Him. He is the Warrior and Hero that we can all fall in love with and follow away from this world that gives nothing back. He is the only real God. Have faith in Him and follow Him out of Egypt, never to return.

# God, where are You leading me today?

# God's Gravitational Pull

*Come near to God and he will come near to you. Wash your hands, you sinners, and purify your hearts, you double-minded.*      ━James 4:8

The sun, being much larger than the earth, has a much stronger gravitational pull. We are not conscious of it because we are so close to the earth and so far from the sun. However, if a spaceship were to be launched out of earth's orbit, it would begin moving toward the sun's gravitational pull. The farther it traveled, the less earth's gravity would affect it and the greater the sun's attraction would become.

"Come near to God and He will come near to you." God wants you to move away from the pull of the world and turn your path toward Him. As your heart draws nearer to God, you will discover that He will draw nearer to you. He and His ways will become increasingly attractive to you. You will become unable to resist His will because His powerful, magnetic, wonderful force is much, much stronger than the world's pull!

# God, where are You leading me today?

February 1

# No One Can Serve Two Masters

*"No servant can serve two masters. Either he will hate the one and love the other, or he will be devoted to the one and despise the other. You cannot serve both God and Money."* ━Luke 16:13

*You cannot drink the cup of the Lord and the cup of demons too; you cannot have a part in both the Lord's table and the table of demons.*

━1 Corinthians 10:21

If you think that you can handle loving both the food and God, you are fooling yourself, but you are not fooling God. No one can serve two masters. I repeat, it is *impossible* to serve two masters. It cannot be done. Our hearts were created to be devoted to only one thing at a time. God is the One who created our hearts this way, so you will never convince Him that you love Him when you are still a slave and servant to the food. Instead, give your heart to the One who created it. Turn your heart against the excess food. Hate the food that your body doesn't need, and instead be fully devoted to God.

The fact that we cannot have two masters is actually very good news for all of us! Once you give your heart to God, you *cannot* give it to food (or any other worldly idol) at the same time! Isn't that wonderful? When your master is the one true God, you will find you will be repulsed by excess food. You will be approaching the Promised Land of having no desire to eat the second half of the plate of food! So, as it is stated in Galatians, if you live by the Spirit, you will not gratify the desires of your sinful nature!

# God, where are You leading me today?

# The Gift of Life

*"Therefore, O house of Israel, I will judge you, each one according to his ways, declares the Sovereign LORD. Repent! Turn away from all your offenses; then sin will not be your downfall. Rid yourselves of all the offenses you have committed, and get a new heart and a new spirit. Why will you die, O house of Israel? For I take no pleasure in the death of anyone, declares the Sovereign LORD. Repent and live!"* ⟶Ezekiel 18:30–32

It is a very nice thing that God has allowed you and me to have our lives. You know, there were many other egg cells and sperm cells for Him to pick from, but God let each of *us* be created and have a heart that beats and loves. It is also a very nice thing that He is giving us a chance to appreciate this life by loving Him first and then letting us enjoy the rest of the earth. With all this in mind, why would you consider loving His earthly creations and putting Him—the Great Creator—on the back burner? It just doesn't make any sense. We should appreciate the wonderful gift of life He has given us, and we should enjoy all the great blessings He has given us here on earth. But above everything else, we should have no other gods before *Him*. He has given us life—so now choose life. Loving Him gives you a new heart and a new spirit!

*February 4*

# God, where are You leading me today?

February 5

# Learn to Expect Temptation

*Be self-controlled and alert. Your enemy the devil prowls around like a roaring lion looking for someone to devour. Resist him, standing firm in the faith, because you know that your brothers throughout the world are undergoing the same kind of sufferings. And the God of all grace, who called you to his eternal glory in Christ, after you have suffered a little while, will himself restore you and make you strong, firm and steadfast.*

*⟶1 Peter 5:8–10*

The world is full of temptations. Everywhere you turn, you can find worldly idols that call for your attention, energy, and worship. Temptations are tough, because they often come when you least expect them. Why would Satan throw a temptation in your path if you are prepared for it and ready to be strong as you turn away? No, Satan waits until you are unsuspecting and content, unprepared to use your strength to turn down the temptation of food, money, sex, or praise. Jesus teaches us in Matthew 6:13 to pray for protection and deliverance from the only being who *can* protect us from the evil one—our heavenly Father: "And lead us not into temptation, but deliver us from the evil one." So learn to expect temptation at each turn, and pray the Lord's prayer daily. God will help you be strong and ready when those worldly temptations pop up!

# God, where are You leading me today?

February 7

# His Name is JEALOUS!

*Do not worship any other god, for the LORD, whose name is Jealous, is a jealous God.* ━━Exodus 34:14

God Himself tells us that He is a jealous God, and yet we ignore this fact. But really take a few minutes and think about it. God is jealous of our hearts beating and racing in excitement for something that is on this earth, or in the heavens above, or in the waters below. Have you ever seen a jealous husband, wife, boyfriend, or girlfriend? They become dangerously jealous when they are afraid their beloved has given his or her heart away to someone else. Well, God displays this same emotion whenever you dream about getting alone with your extra food or other stronghold for a secret rendezvous. Anger and love are actually very near one another. It makes my heart break for Him when I think about the many times He has gotten angry throughout the history of mankind because we are kissing something on this earth. We shouldn't think that He doesn't mind—after all, we have learned from His own Word that He is a jealous God . . . His name is JEALOUS!

# God, where are You leading me today?

February 9

# Love God and Enjoy His Food

*And God spoke all these words: "I am the LORD your God, who brought you out of Egypt, out of the land of slavery. You shall have no other gods before me."* ◆━Exodus 20:1–3

While God has put all foods on earth for us to enjoy, it is a very sad fact that many Christians are *loving* the food ... and are only *enjoying* God. Being overweight seems to have become very accepted among churchgoers. In fact, many Bible studies and fellowship activities revolve around the food that is served. Again, God means for us to enjoy His wonderful variety of foods, but I'm here to tell you the truth: we must stop loving the food and just enjoying God! Reverse this! *Love God* ... and enjoy His food.

When we seek God first, a relationship is birthed, but God pulls back from the heart of the one who chooses other gods to adore. How could we have ever put God in second place? My friends, this cannot be. It is one thing to be caught red-handed one time with another lover—food—but many of us are repeatedly choosing to embrace it—sometimes secretly, other times in public. Many of us even joke about it. We even bring our secret loves into the only place in this world that is not supposed to have the world in it, the only place on earth where God asks for it to be just you and Him—your heart. Remember God's commandment to have no other gods before Him, and start today loving Him *first* and thankfully enjoying His many blessings on earth.

# God, where are You leading me today?

February 11

# Stop Working on Obedience—Start Working on Love

*"If anyone loves me, he will obey my teaching. My Father will love him, and we will come to him and make our home with him. He who does not love me will not obey my teaching. These words you hear are not my own; they belong to the Father who sent me."* —John 14: 23–24

If you love, love, love the Father and His precious son Jesus Christ, then you will not have any trouble obeying the Father today. It won't be work to obey, but it will be a joy! After all, what boss could ever be more loving or more powerful or more all-knowing? Once you realize His love for you and recognize all the things He does for you each and every day, you will fall in love with Him. You will start seeing His works everywhere, and the invisible God will become more visible to you. But you must give your heart to Him in love first, and then the obedience to His commands will come naturally. So stop working on the obedience, and start working on *loving God* today. You will feel the changes in your heart, and before you know it, you will want to obey His commands. In fact, it will be easy and fun!

*February 12*

# God, where are You leading me today?

---

*February 13*

# Exposing the False God of Food

*Trust in the LORD and do good; dwell in the land and enjoy safe pasture.*
*Delight yourself in the LORD and he will give you the desires of your heart.*
*—Psalm 37: 3–4*

How can you leave food or other strongholds behind and dwell in the safe pasture of the Lord? Well, how did the children of God leave Egypt? There are two things you need to know. Number one: Open your eyes to what a life-sucking leech the god of food is and what a life-replenisher God is. Number two: Take a crash course on how to fall in love with God.

First, let's expose this false god called food, so that you can fall out of love with it. Just how good has excessive food been to you? Has bowing down to extra food helped your finances? No, it robs you as you spend more and more on food and diet plans. Has food clothed you? No, you probably find less and less to wear as you obey food more and more. Has it helped your self-esteem? No, the more that excessive food gathers on your hips and in other locations of the body, the more your self-esteem drops. Does it help your relationships? No, it often puts a wedge between you and your family or spouse. Does it help your looks? No, in fact, being overweight distorts the looks that God gave you. So you see, the god of food turns out to be a false, parasitic leech that robs you of time, passion, money, devotion, peace, and self-esteem. It is a false master that leaves you with increasing troubles, guilt, emotional deprivation, and physical ailments. It cannot give back to you or return your love.

Now, you need to realize what a loving, generous, pow-

*February 14*

erful, and attractive God our true Lord is. He can provide anything and everything for you. He can lift your self-esteem, fix your finances, and strengthen your relationships. He is the One True God, and falling in love with Him will give you real peace and contentment as you finally realize the desires of your heart.

God, where are You leading me today?

# Obedience Follows Love

*Do not merely listen to the word, and so deceive yourselves. Do what it says.* —James 1:22

We know we should obey God, but what exactly does that mean? We can all go through the actions of obedience, but how can we truly change for good? Well, real change starts in your head, then drops to your heart, and then the body follows. If you choose to love God above all other things, it will be easy to serve Him or obey Him. In fact, it will be impossible to *stop* serving Him—that is the behavior of love. You can't work your way to heaven, and you can't just go through the actions. If you love Him, you will obey Him. Stop working on the obedience, and start working on the love. The obedience will just naturally follow. Fix the heart, and your body will lose the weight permanently. That's when you know you've got it!

# God, where are You leading me today?

February 17

# Treasure His Words

*I have treasured the words of his mouth more than my daily bread.*
*—Job 23:12b*

*Your statutes are wonderful; therefore I obey them. The unfolding of your words gives light; it gives understanding to the simple. I open my mouth and pant, longing for your commands. Turn to me and have mercy on me, as you always do to those who love your name. Direct my footsteps according to your word; let no sin rule over me. Redeem me from the oppression of men, that I may obey your precepts. Make your face shine upon your servant and teach me your decrees. Streams of tears flow from my eyes, for your law is not obeyed.* *—Psalm 119: 129–136*

I feel like Job in the first scripture above, because I do treasure the words of God's mouth more than my daily bread. I do not have just a one-way relationship with the Father. I have a two-way conversation, even though I do not hear a voice audibly. I stay in the Word to hear His voice. I have several Bibles that I like to use that are all identical. I found out that these Bibles are called "church pew Bibles" because they are actually the plain Bibles found on the back of a pew to use during the worship service. I was really proud of my favorite Bibles until I found out they were just the plain Bibles that are used when you forget to bring your own to church! No matter what the Bible looks like on the outside, though, I treasure each and every word inside.

The only time I panic is when I think I have left my Bible at home after leaving on a trip. God's guidance is everything to me, and I want to know what He thinks. He keeps my foot from stumbling, He gives me wisdom for which direction to turn, and He protects me from the enemy. I have to have His Word, and I love His laws because they are always right! There is no principle that you have a question about that is not answered in God's Word.

*February 18*

# God, where are You leading me today?

February 19

# For Yours Is the Kingdom

*"Our Father in heaven, hallowed be your name,*
*your kingdom come, your will be done on earth as it is in heaven.*
*Give us today our daily bread.*
*Forgive us our debts, as we also have forgiven our debtors.*
*And lead us not into temptation, but deliver us from the evil one."*
*—Matthew 6:9b-13*

Jesus taught us how to pray, and I believe His heart was saying the following:
Dear Heavenly Father:

*Hallowed be Your name.* (Hallowed and awesome and incredible and most deserving be Your Name; You are a Genius beyond genius.)

*Your kingdom come.* (We pray that Your ideas, Your truths, Your government, Your justice, and Your ways to live replace this worldly way of life because Your kingdom is perfect.)

*Give us today our daily bread.* (Give us this day the portion we need.)

*Lead us not into temptation.* (May we not be tempted today. After all, this is not our kingdom—it is Yours.)

*And deliver us from the evil one.* (Deliver us from Satan, who is constantly misrepresenting You and falsely accusing You. We know that You are perfect in all Your leadership.)

For Yours is the kingdom, the power, and the glory forever. (After all, You are It. You are everything. You are all-powerful. You are who we worship, admire, and adore.)

Amen.

# God, where are You leading me today?

# The Created versus the Creator

*They exchanged the truth of God for a lie, and worshiped and served created things rather than the Creator—who is forever praised. Amen.*
*—Romans 1:25*

There is a human tendency to worship the *created* and not the *Creator*. We worship things because of the temporary pleasures they give us, but we ignore the One who made us capable of feeling that pleasure. We are so quick to fall in love with an object because of its beauty or its capability, but we fail to recognize that the Father created that beauty and that capability even before the object was formed.

God is jealous of our attention to and adoration of the things that He has made. How can we get so confused that we forget that it is God who made everything on this earth? It is He who made our senses so that we could experience and celebrate His genius, and He gave us these things on earth to enjoy. Let's stop being confused and start showing God our appreciation instead of ignoring Him in favor of His creations.

# God, where are You leading me today?

February 23

# A Superior Invitation

*What then? Shall we sin because we are not under law but under grace? By no means! Don't you know that when you offer yourselves to someone to obey him as slaves, you are slaves to the one whom you obey—whether you are slaves to sin, which leads to death, or to obedience, which leads to righteousness? But thanks be to God that, though you used to be slaves to sin, you wholeheartedly obeyed the form of teaching to which you were entrusted. You have been set free from sin and have become slaves to righteousness.*

*~Romans 6:15–18*

Grace should not be abused, and we should not embarrass God in front of all the celestial world by running after other lovers on this earth. We have the opportunity, given through God's grace and mercy alone, to accept a covenant offered by God that is similar to a marriage proposal. He has made the offer and the provisions through Jesus Christ to cross the tracks, since we live on the wrong side of the tracks. Through Jesus Christ, we can approach the throne and have the opportunity to be an employee of the most powerful CEO in the universe. What we do to chase down the best mate . . . what we do to get the best job—open your eyes: you've been offered both! No longer run after other things—run after God. That's how to accept grace and no longer continue in sin. It's that simple! Accept His kind proposal. Put your hands to the plow and do *not* look back.

# God, where are You leading me today?

February 25

# A Sign of His Goodness

*Turn to me and have mercy on me; grant your strength to your servant and save the son of your maidservant. Give me a sign of your goodness, that my enemies may see it and be put to shame, for you, O LORD, have helped me and comforted me.* ══►*Psalm 86:16–17*

It is okay to call out to God and ask Him to show you that He is there for you. There are times when we all need this reassurance. It is also okay to call upon Him for your needs. After all, He wants you to see His glorious works for you, so that you will experience the direct relationship between your request and His answer. This will help you develop pure trust that He can and will take care of you. Ask for a sign of His goodness today, and be prepared to be awed!

Physical reassurance builds our faith. I have never found God to get upset when we ask for evidence of His love; however, scriptures indicate that God does not like unbelievers to *keep* asking for signs to prove His existence (Matthew 16:1–4). How annoying that must be to God! We see the stars, His handiwork, His sunsets that have a different color scheme daily, and we witness the birth of new life. Yet some *still* demand a miraculous sign to prove the existence of God. Please! God is tired of showing off in such fantastic ways and having people still demand a sign to prove His existence. But for the person pursuing a loving relationship with God, He provides whatever it takes to make His beloved secure in His presence. Asking for reassurance from God is not testing God—it is *seeking* God. That is His command for us.

# God, where are You leading me today?

February 27

# No Middle Ground

*Do not love the world or anything in the world. If anyone loves the world, the love of the Father is not in him.* —*1 John 2:15*

Moses cried out in Deuteronomy 30 that there were only two choices, and he called them "life" and "death." Ezekiel pointed out that there were only two choices: righteousness and unrighteousness. The writer of Hebrews made sure that we understood that there were only two categories: the obedient and the disobedient, the believer and the unbeliever. The Apostle John wrote of only two types of people: those who love and those who hate. And finally, God Himself gave us two choices in Exodus 20: hate Him or love Him. Never, in any of these categories, is there even the slightest hint of an unattached or lukewarm option. There is no middle ground. All throughout the Old and New Testaments, God gets upset at His children for even turning to another lover, much less trying to talk Him into letting all *three* into the same relationship. That is analogous to asking your spouse to allow you to have a second lover in bed with him! This is unthinkable—especially to such a wonderful God. Make the choice to turn to Him and give Him your heart for good.

# God, where are You leading me today?

_March 1_

# Desert Journey

# Step Out in Faith

*He led you through the vast and dreadful desert, that thirsty and waterless land, with its venomous snakes and scorpions.* —*Deuteronomy 8:15a*

The desert is described in the Bible as "vast and dreadful, thirsty and waterless, with snakes and scorpions." As you entered this place and things started to get tough, many of you were tempted to return to Egypt and the slavery of dieting. In the beginning, you learned that your *mind* was focused on food more than you knew. Then, you found out that your *heart* was given to food, too. How do I know? Because in my years of counseling, I've learned that everyone has felt the tug-of-war—the major battles going on for the heart. If you had just been missing information, one week would have done it. But you never realized that making a choice to turn to God was going to be such a heart-stopper. My advice—just step out in faith, as you would on a blind date. God will be better than a binge, but you have to go out and taste and see that He is good. And to do that, you have to leave some food behind and step into the desert.

# God, where are You leading me today?

March 3

# Obey the Lord's Order

*Whenever the cloud lifted from above the Tent, the Israelites set out; wherever the cloud settled, the Israelites encamped. At the LORD's command the Israelites set out, and at his command they encamped. As long as the cloud stayed over the tabernacle, they remained in camp. When the cloud remained over the tabernacle a long time, the Israelites obeyed the LORD's order and did not set out. Sometimes the cloud was over the tabernacle only a few days; at the LORD's command they would encamp, and then at his command they would set out. Sometimes the cloud stayed only from evening till morning, and when it lifted in the morning, they set out. Whether by day or by night, whenever the cloud lifted, they set out. Whether the cloud stayed over the tabernacle for two days or a month or a year, the Israelites would remain in camp and not set out; but when it lifted, they would set out. At the LORD's command they encamped, and at the LORD's command they set out. They obeyed the LORD's order, in accordance with his command through Moses.*
*◄ Numbers 9:17–23*

After the parting of the Red Sea, the children of God followed the cloud by day and the fire by night. No matter whether the cloud stayed two days or a month or a year, the Israelites would remain in camp. But when the cloud lifted, they would set out again. Think about this if you start feeling sorry that you have to look to God to know when you are hungry and when you are full. The Israelites had to look up *all day* and *all night.* Even in the middle of the night, they had to pack their tents, put out the fires, gather the children and pets, and take off. Sometimes, just after they had unpacked their belongings, set up the tent, and had a good pot of manna boiling, God lifted the cloud and they had to pack everything up and take off again. We should stop complaining about the red light and green light of hunger. All *you* will have to pack up is a carryout of food!

*March 4*

# God, where are You leading me today?

March 5

# God Hears Our Cries

*Then they cried out to the LORD in their trouble, and he delivered them from their distress.* —Psalm 107:6

At one time, God's children were free men in a foreign land. But once God saw they had become slaves and were forced to make bricks for Egypt, He heard their cries, and He fought a mighty battle for the deliverance of the Israelites. God is now fighting for the deliverance of your heart so that you will no longer experience an attraction to things on this earth. He can deliver your heart from the distress of any addiction, because His attraction is much stronger than the earth's attraction. You just need to cry out to God to rescue you and keep your eyes focused on Him, and you will experience His mighty deliverance.

# God, where are You leading me today?

March 7

# God Speaks Tenderly to Us

*"Therefore I am now going to allure her; I will lead her into the desert and speak tenderly to her. There I will give her back her vineyards, and will make the Valley of Achor a door of hope. There she will sing as in the days of her youth, as in the day she came up out of Egypt. In that day," declares the* LORD, *"you will call me 'my husband'; you will no longer call me 'my master.' I will remove the names of the Baals from her lips; no longer will their names be invoked."* ⟶*Hosea 2:14–17*

When you turn back to God and away from the food, God will reward you. He will turn your past troubles into a door of hope and happiness. You see, God is a genius of behavior modification. He knows that as humans, we would rather do the things that will bring us happiness . . . and what better happiness and peace than can be offered by the Creator of the universe? Our loving Father loves to reward us when we choose to spend time adoring and worshiping Him instead of mere earthly things. God wants to allure us, to lead us, and to speak tenderly to us. What earthly idol can compare to that? When you fall in love with God, you will no longer call for your stronghold. In that way, God removes the names of your idols from your lips.

# God, where are You leading me today?

*March 9*

# You Are Not a God

*This is what the Sovereign LORD says: "In the pride of your heart you say, 'I am a god; I sit on the throne of a god in the heart of the seas.' But you are a man and not a god, though you think you are as wise as a god."*

*—Ezekiel 28:2b*

Face it. If something is going wrong, you have become your own boss again. The Bible tells us that if we remain connected to God, everything we need will be given to us. So if things are going wrong, let this be a sign to you to reexamine your relationship with the Father. Don't you want to let Him guide you today? If you do, you will find happiness. After all, God knows the past, present, and future, and He loves you and wants the best for you. Who better to give you advice? You will be such good friends with God when you let Him *be* God. Then you can ask Him for anything you want, and He will give it. It is so fun!

*March 10*

# God, where are You leading me today?

March 11

# An Even Greater Enemy than Pharaoh

*For the LORD brought you out of Egypt with his mighty hand.*
*Exodus 13:9b*

God rescued the Israelites from the slavery of this earth, and what a battle it was! He took them into the desert so He could win the heart of man with no earthly competition. However, He found that the desert brought forth a more ominous competition—the god of self. The Israelites kept crying out, "Why have you brought us up out of Egypt to die in the desert? Why have you brought us up out of Egypt to die in the desert?" That is the point exactly: God brought them out to die . . . *to die to their wills*. But the desert only seemed to revive the will of man, even making it stronger than it was while under the burden of slavery to the earth!

The will of man was thriving, not dying as planned. Suffering in the desert was not killing the craving of man. Many of you have found a greater battle going on in the desert than you have ever felt before. The will of man seems to have an independent heartbeat of its own, and it has no intention of learning trust in the one true Lord as long as this little god's heart is beating. What foolish pride we have! But the cloud of God stayed over the rebellious hearts of the Israelites, patiently watching to see if anyone would consider joining the kingdom of which He is the boss.

*March 12*

# God, where are You leading me today?

# Food Is Not Your Boss

*But now that you have been set free from sin and have become slaves to God, the benefit you reap leads to holiness, and the result is eternal life.*
*—Romans 6:22*

Romans 6:16 tells us that we are slaves to the one whom we obey. Up until now, you have been a slave to food, or money, or sexual lust, or sports, or television. But what a wonderful opportunity you now have! You have been set free—you are no longer a slave to any of these worldly things. When food or anything of the world calls your name today, you can say, "No! *You* are not my boss!" What a great freedom to have only one Master, our awesome God Almighty! The result is life—so, get a life!

*March 14*

# God, where are You leading me today?

March 15

# Guard Your Soul

*In the paths of the wicked lie thorns and snares, but he who **guards** his soul stays far from them.* ━Proverbs 22:5

*Rejoice in the Lord always. I will say it again: Rejoice! Let your gentleness be evident to all. The Lord is near. Do not be anxious about anything, but in everything, by prayer and petition, with thanksgiving, present your requests to God. And the peace of God, which transcends all understanding, will **guard** your hearts and your minds in Christ Jesus.* ━Philippians 4:4–7

Guard your heart from evil thoughts. Make sure your heart and mind do not linger on thoughts that will lead you astray. Sin can take root in our hearts and grow strong if we are not careful. Remember in Mark 7:20–23, Jesus said: "What comes out of a man is what makes him 'unclean.' For from within, out of men's hearts, come evil thoughts, sexual immorality, theft, murder, adultery, greed, malice, deceit, lewdness, envy, slander, arrogance and folly. All these evils come from inside and make a man 'unclean.'" So we should always be careful to protect ourselves within. Set your mind on things above. Keep your heart busy by focusing on God's business and what He is doing, and you will reap great reward. Be careful, eyes, what you see, and be careful, ears, what you hear.

*March 16*

# God, where are You leading me today?

March 17

# The Lord Will Fight for You

*As Pharaoh approached, the Israelites looked up, and there were the Egyptians, marching after them. They were terrified and cried out to the LORD. Moses answered the people, "Do not be afraid. Stand firm and you will see the deliverance the LORD will bring you today. The Egyptians you see today you will never see again. The LORD will fight for you; you need only to be still." Then the LORD said to Moses, "Why are you crying out to me? Tell the Israelites to move on. Raise your staff and stretch out your hand over the sea to divide the water so that the Israelites can go through the sea on dry ground."* ⸺*Exodus 14:10,13–16*

When Satan comes in with his temptations and attacks, trying to lure you back to Egypt, stand firm and call out to God. Do not plan to defend yourself. Just run to God and watch *Him* defeat the enemy. He will defend you. Quit worrying about Egypt and the Egyptians and Satan, for you'll never see them again if you allow God to defend you. If you are spending your energy living in fear of the attacks of Satan, then you are not focused on God. You can't be in both camps. Now, if you want to enter the desert, what do you need to do? You need to move on! Get going! Pursue God with all your might, and He will lead you safely.

*March 18*

# God, where are You leading me today?

March 19

# "Esau I Hated"

*Just as it is written: "Jacob I loved, but Esau I hated."* —Romans 9:13
*See that no one . . . is godless like Esau, who for a single meal sold his inheritance rights as the oldest son.* —Hebrews 12:16

When I was a young girl, I wondered what it meant when God said, "Jacob I loved, but Esau I hated." Did Jacob not lie and cheat to get his brother's birthright? Is that okay with God? As I got older, I understood this better. Now I understand that Jacob was crazy about God, and he would even cheat and lie to obtain the birthright, because this inheritance would make him even closer to God. Esau, on the other hand, was willing to sell this priceless birthright for a simple bowl of stew! Think about it: Esau traded being close to God for food! Does this sound familiar to you? Esau is even called "godless" in Hebrews, where we are cautioned not to be like him.

God loves the child who wants to get closer to Him or get in good with Him, and He will reward your efforts. I do not get mad at my dogs, Chaucer and Virginia, for fighting over getting close to me. God loved Jacob for doing everything he could to get close to God's heart. To most people, Esau looks sinless and Jacob looks like a sinner. But think again. Sin is not loving God fully and wholeheartedly, and it can be manifested in many ways—just as seeking the Father can be.

*March 20*

# God, where are You leading me today?

March 21

# Love God First, Then Everyone Else

*This is the message you heard from the beginning: We should love one another. Do not be like Cain, who belonged to the evil one and murdered his brother. And why did he murder him? Because his own actions were evil and his brother's were righteous. Do not be surprised, my brothers, if the world hates you. We know that we have passed from death to life, because we love our brothers. Anyone who does not love remains in death. Anyone who hates his brother is a murderer, and you know that no murderer has eternal life in him. This is how we know what love is: Jesus Christ laid down his life for us. And we ought to lay down our lives for our brothers.*

*—1 John 3:11–16*

God has shown us clearly through the Ten Command-ments that He wants us to love and honor Him above all else. Jesus stated that we should love God, and then love our fellow man as ourselves—in that order. You see, when you have the relationship in which God is your heart's foremost desire, then, and only then, can you love and honor mankind the way you should. After all, if you love God and believe that He created and cares for everyone on the earth, how could you hurt one of the children that He loves? That would just be unnatural!

# God, where are You leading me today?

March 23

# The Greatest Defender

*The LORD says to my Lord: "Sit at my right hand until I make your enemies a footstool for your feet."* ⬛~*Psalm 110:1*

*Do not take revenge, my friends, but leave room for God's wrath, for it is written: "It is mine to avenge; I will repay," says the Lord.* ⬛~*Romans 12:19*

Instead of trying to defend yourself, let God defend you. I have witnessed God setting my enemies down over and over. I define an enemy as one who attacks me as I try to serve the Lord and follow His will. If the enemy can make you look bad or falsely accuse you in front of others, then the attack can potentially stop God's sheep from seeing the truth about how easy it is to come to the Father. God certainly does not want this to happen.

I have seen God fight. He is a brilliant strategist and the best of the best generals in war. Enemies of those who truly love God should watch out, for it is God's to avenge, and He will repay! Keep your battle armor on, but let God do the avenging.

# God, where are You leading me today?

March 25

# The Stomach God

*Join with others in following my example, brothers, and take note of those who live according to the pattern we gave you. For, as I have often told you before and now say again even with tears, many live as enemies of the cross of Christ. Their destiny is destruction, their god is their stomach, and their glory is in their shame. Their mind is on earthly things. But our citizenship is in heaven. And we eagerly await a Savior from there, the Lord Jesus Christ, who, by the power that enables him to bring everything under his control, will transform our lowly bodies so that they will be like his glorious body.*
*⸺Philippians 3:17–21*

An enemy of the cross of Christ has his stomach as his god. Does this hit home? Don't let your stomach be your god. You will only get larger and larger with this type of worship. And as you grow larger, so will your desire; it will never be satisfied. And think about it: your *stomach*—what a stupid god to bow down to! People who do this run over others as they lust and live for the "feedings" every day. Focus off your stomach, and just let it do the job God meant for it to do. Instead, focus on the wonderful spiritual food that God provides—the satisfying nutrition of an interactive relationship with Him! Take hold of your citizenship in heaven, and mold your heart to be more like our heavenly Father.

# God, where are You leading me today?

*March 27*

# What Do You Worry About?

*"Who of you by worrying can add a single hour to his life? And why do you worry about clothes? See how the lilies of the field grow. They do not labor or spin. Yet I tell you that not even Solomon in all his splendor was dressed like one of these. If that is how God clothes the grass of the field, which is here today and tomorrow is thrown into the fire, will he not much more clothe you, O you of little faith? So do not worry, saying, 'What shall we eat?' or 'What shall we drink?' or 'What shall we wear?' For the pagans run after all these things, and your heavenly Father knows that you need them. But seek first his kingdom and his righteousness, and all these things will be given to you as well. Therefore do not worry about tomorrow, for tomorrow will worry about itself. Each day has enough trouble of its own."*

*━Matthew 6:27–34*

What you worry about is your idol. Do you worry about your children, or your spouse, or your own health? These are common idols. Shift that worry and concern and energy into worrying about God's children more than your own children. Most of God's children are lost and very underfed, or even emaciated, spiritually. Their spiritual health is the worst. They are dying of spiritual cancers that are taking over the heart, and they have spiritually clogged arteries. Make *this* your worry and God will be sure to please you beyond what you could think or imagine or dream. All you ever wanted for your family will come to be!

*March 28*

# God, where are You leading me today?

March 29

# Keeping God Near

*Righteous are you, O LORD, and your laws are right. The statutes you have laid down are righteous; they are fully trustworthy. My zeal wears me out, for my enemies ignore your words. Your promises have been thoroughly tested, and your servant loves them. Though I am lowly and despised, I do not forget your precepts. Your righteousness is everlasting and your law is true. Trouble and distress have come upon me, but your commands are my delight. Your statutes are forever right; give me understanding that I may live.* ▬Psalm 119:137–144

King David was always thinking about God, whether he was praying to Him or singing songs of appreciation, joy, and even sorrow to Him. We, too, should meditate on God's law all day long. One way to do this is to keep God's Word by you at all times. I keep a copy of the Bible everywhere I go, and my heart quickens when I think I can get some time alone with God. I talk to Him all the time, not just in formal prayers. No matter who I am with or where I am, I know that God would come if I needed Him, and I know that He keeps angels nearby. Trust in God's superior knowledge and love, and—like King David—have faith that His guidance will make you wiser.

# God, where are You leading me today?

_____
_____
_____
_____
_____
_____
_____
_____
_____
_____
_____
_____
_____
_____
_____
_____
_____
_____
_____
_____
_____
_____
_____
_____
_____
_____

*March 31*

# John the Baptist Prepares the Way

*In those days John the Baptist came, preaching in the Desert of Judea and saying, "Repent, for the kingdom of heaven is near." This is he who was spoken of through the prophet Isaiah: "A voice of one calling in the desert, 'Prepare the way for the Lord, make straight paths for him.'"*

*—Matthew 3:1–3*

When John the Baptist came and told people how to prepare for heaven, he told them to *repent*. John was preparing the way for the Lord by telling people to repent. Why is repentance so important? Well, repentance is not only the key to unlocking the heart of *man*, but it is also the key to unlocking *God's* heartstrings. True repentance unlocks the heart of man by cleaning out the heart of its impurities, making it humble and open to God's commands in recognition of the Lord's sovereignty. True repentance unlocks God's heartstrings in the same way. It shows God that you are ready to accept His will and His decisions and His commands. It says to God, "I know that You are the best for me, and I want to throw away my impurities and serve You in obedience." Your heart cannot house your old goals *and* your new goals. Repent, and have one sweet goal: following Jesus Christ all the way to the heart of the Father!

*April 1*

# God, where are You leading me today?

April 2

# God Is Your Everything

*He said to me: "It is done. I am the Alpha and the Omega, the Beginning and the End. To him who is thirsty I will give to drink without cost from the spring of the water of life. He who overcomes will inherit all this, and I will be his God and he will be my son."* —*Revelation 21:6–7*

*And my God will meet all your needs according to his glorious riches in Christ Jesus.* —*Philippians 4:19*

Our days are so busy. We work, we raise a family, we have so many things we do each day. We spend a lot of time worrying about all the things we need to do, but we really shouldn't worry. When you are focused on God and looking to Him to help do your job, help raise the children, and help with your marriage, then you will experience how He takes care of everything you have been worried about. If you give everything to God, including every daily activity and worry, He will provide for you in large ways and small ways. You will find that suddenly it seems like you are able to achieve so much more than you thought you could. If you stay focused on God, you will find that He is your *Alpha* and *Omega*. He is the beginning and the end. He is everything and provides everything!

*April 3*

# God, where are You leading me today?

_April 4_

# "Each One Is to Gather as Much as He Needs"

*"This is what the LORD has commanded: 'Each one is to gather as much as he needs . . . .'" Then Moses said to them, "No one is to keep any of it until morning." However, some of them paid no attention to Moses; they kept part of it until morning, but it was full of maggots and began to smell. So Moses was angry with them.* ━Exodus 16:16a ,19–20

Food was made to be a tool to serve mankind, not man to be the slave of food! It is not wrong to leave food behind on your plate. If it rots or is wasted, so what! God has more for you. When God sent the Israelites manna to eat in the desert, He sent them more than they needed to be satisfied. But He told them not to be greedy and not to gather more than they needed for that day. Notice that the Lord commanded each to gather as much as he *needs*, not as much as his head wants or as much as his neighbor gathers. We need to trust God to provide our daily bread, which He will provide each and every day. Do not show a lack of faith in His completely competent care by being greedy or by getting yourself extra food as if there will be no food for tomorrow. Do not let yourself or your children be a slave to leftovers. Let's learn from the Israelites' example—have faith that God will give you what you need.

*April 5*

# God, where are You leading me today?

April 6

# Cloud by Day, Fire by Night

*By day the LORD went ahead of them in a pillar of cloud to guide them on their way and by night in a pillar of fire to give them light, so that they could travel by day or night. Neither the pillar of cloud by day nor the pillar of fire by night left its place in front of the people.* ⟶*Exodus 13:21–22*

*But when he, the Spirit of truth, comes, he will guide you into all truth. He will not speak on his own; he will speak only what he hears, and he will tell you what is yet to come.* ⟶*John 16:13*

Once God parted the Red Sea and delivered the Israelites from the slavery of Egypt, scripture tells us that He went ahead of them in the form of a cloud by day and a fire by night. This cloud never left their side the entire 40 years of the desert, no matter what they did to God—and they did some pretty wicked things. God is still with us today—actually even closer than the cloud, since He has sent the Holy Spirit to us to guide us into all truths. How attentive can you get? No other being has been so kind, and because of His personal care, I love Him! Open up all of your senses to learn His leading.

# God, where are You leading me today?

April 8

# Feeding His Lambs

*When they had finished eating, Jesus said to Simon Peter, "Simon son of John, do you truly love me more than these?" "Yes, Lord," he said, "you know that I love you." Jesus said, "Feed my lambs." Again Jesus said, "Simon son of John, do you truly love me?" He answered, "Yes, Lord, you know that I love you." Jesus said, "Take care of my sheep." The third time he said to him, "Simon son of John, do you love me?" Peter was hurt because Jesus asked him the third time, "Do you love me?" He said, "Lord, you know all things; you know that I love you." Jesus said, "Feed my sheep." —John 21:15-17*

So what is the key to showing our love for the Father? The answer is here: Focus on God and His sheep. Jesus wants His lambs . . . His followers . . . those who are seeking to know more about Him . . . to be fed and not to go hungry for the knowledge of Him or for His love. Jesus wants each of us who love and care for Him to love and care for others in the world, for *all* are His lambs. In fact, we should be more concerned about feeding His sheep than feeding ourselves, for we know that God will take care of us! We have already learned from Jesus that if we love God, we will obey His commands. Obey the above command He gave to Simon, and then write to me (the address can be found in the back of this book) and let me know of the secret heartfelt joy this focus brings to you today!

# God, where are You leading me today?

April 10

# Are You Backstroking the Red Sea?

*Therefore, prepare your minds for action; be self-controlled; set your hope fully on the grace to be given you when Jesus Christ is revealed. As obedient children, do not conform to the evil desires you had when you lived in ignorance. But just as he who called you is holy, so be holy in all you do; for it is written: "Be holy, because I am holy."*　　　　*━1 Peter 1:13–16*

If we find ourselves in the pantry and refrigerator night after night, we are still in the arms of Egypt. But I'm afraid the deceiver has told us that we have made God our choice and that we have left our slavery. Even after the mighty Exodus, many of us have slowly done the backstroke across the Red Sea and wound up back on the shoreline of Egypt. We are actually back in Egypt—but this time, it's been redecorated so that we will not recognize it. Where once there were pyramids, there are now church pews and stained-glass windows. We have brought the world into the church, the one place where it should only be us and God. Listen to what Peter wrote: "As obedient children, do not conform to the evil desires you had when you lived in ignorance." Do not backstroke across the Red Sea to Egypt's shore. We need to start now to help clean up the church (and our hearts) for God!

*April 11*

# God, where are You leading me today?

April 12

# Welcoming the Father

*An argument started among the disciples as to which of them would be the greatest. Jesus, knowing their thoughts, took a little child and had him stand beside him. Then he said to them, "Whoever welcomes this little child in my name welcomes me; and whoever welcomes me welcomes the one who sent me. For he who is least among you all—he is the greatest."*

*—Luke 9:46–48*

This passage simply means that the less you think you have and the more you rely on God, the more you will get. The one who is least usually has no problem with trying to be a god and has no problem with pride. These are the conditions that will leave room for the holy and separate spirit of God to come in and not mix with your own spirit. So if we welcome the little ones into the kingdom, then we are welcoming the Father in!

In Luke 10:21b, Jesus becomes full of joy through the Holy Spirit, and He proclaims, "I praise you, Father, Lord of heaven and earth, because you have hidden these things from the wise and learned, and revealed them to little children. Yes, Father, for this was your good pleasure." I just love this passage because it shows the love God has for the priceless heart. People who have no need for God cannot please God. Those of us who know that we need Him every hour of every day are like the little children. The heart of a child is the heart that fits right in with the perfectly powerful but humble kingdom of God.

*April 13*

# God, where are You leading me today?

April 14

# Sinking and Saving

*But when he saw the wind, he was afraid and, beginning to sink, cried out, "Lord, save me!" Immediately Jesus reached out his hand and caught him. "You of little faith," he said, "why did you doubt?"* —Matthew 14:30–31

If you trust God to feed you, you naturally will not focus on the food at all. A person could *believe* that God will provide . . . but to *trust* Him fully means that you are happy with the amount of food He gives you. You trust that this amount is the best for your heart, soul, and body, even if the amount is a lot smaller than you would have chosen for yourself. The person who does *not* fully trust God to provide, however, will feel obligated to focus back on the food all throughout the day. The next thing you know, he is unsure about weight loss and is back on the scales; he grows uneasy about eating regular foods, and he is back to counting fat grams and calories. This lack of trust in God's total reign could send you back down a path of slavery. If that happens, you will find that you have totally lost your focus, and like Peter, you are sinking in the water. Follow Peter's example—call out to Jesus to save you. Your sinking and His saving are part of the process that Jesus will allow as He trains you in obedience.

*April 15*

# God, where are You leading me today?

*April 16*

# Arrogant, Overfed, and Unconcerned

*"Now this was the sin of your sister Sodom: She and her daughters were arrogant, overfed and unconcerned; they did not help the poor and needy. They were haughty and did detestable things before me. Therefore I did away with them as you have seen."* —Ezekiel 16:49–50

I believe there are many obstacles to overcome when you turn your whole heart purely to the Father. But nothing worries me more than the attitude of *unconcern*. People who don't know the truth don't even have the opportunity to surface an unconcerned attitude. But once you have been told the truth about your heart wandering to food, then you should feel saddened and guilty, much like the thief on the cross who said, "We deserve what we are getting." The book of Ezekiel marries the word "unconcerned" with *overfed*. Something tells me if we would not overeat, then we would develop more and more concern about our relationship with the Father. When we release our heart from being enslaved to an idol, we can give our heart to Whom it belongs: to God. The last associated word is *arrogant*. You probably do not consider yourself arrogant, but if you have remained overweight for a while, you *do* have all of these qualities because you think you don't need to obey God like other people do. You consider yourself special. But believe me—arrogant, overfed, and unconcerned is *not* where you want to be. Join me and many others and change your heart today!

# God, where are You leading me today?

April 18

# Try Him and See

*"Test me in this," says the LORD Almighty, "and see if I will not throw open the floodgates of heaven and pour out so much blessing that you will not have room enough for it."* ➤Malachi 3:10b

We cannot run to false gods to get us out of our pain, and we cannot save ourselves by building golden calves in the form of diet pills, liposuction, diet programs, hospital liquid diets, and fat farms. Let's get serious by giving our heart, our soul, our mind, and our strength to obeying *God* rather than food. We need to develop a relationship with God the Father through Jesus Christ. That is the only way we can come to trust that He truly is the One who can rescue us from our troubles. Then, the next thing we know, we are falling in love with Him. We will forget our old love called food. When we give everything to Him, our true God, He takes our heart, our soul, our mind, and our strength and multiplies them a hundred times and gives them back to us. Just as the false god robs you, the true God gives back great dividends. You give Him the rest of your sandwich; He gives you back the next smaller dress or pants size, along with many other jewels. He is a multibillionaire! You cannot outgive the one true God. Just try Him and see! He *is* the God to follow, and He will pour out blessings for you when you give yourself totally to Him.

*April 19*

# God, where are You leading me today?

April 20

# Vessels Cannot Be Lazy

*The sluggard says, "There is a lion in the road, a fierce lion roaming the streets!" As a door turns on its hinges, so a sluggard turns on his bed. The sluggard buries his hand in the dish; he is too lazy to bring it back to his mouth.* ━Proverbs 26:13–15

We cannot be lazy or lukewarm for God, or we are failing to glorify Him. For example, how could a lazy bird glorify God? If the bird was programmed by God to fly high, then the bird should obey and soar to great heights in the sky. If butterflies are programmed to migrate thousands of miles and keep the same mate, then God is glorified when this is carried out. A butterfly that doesn't meet its full God-given potential is not allowing God to be a good ruler over subjects who are happy to obey His command. Outsiders could wrongfully conclude that God is a dictator—someone asking for too much from His subjects and whose subjects probably don't like Him anyway. The creations of God who are lazy prevent the invisible God from becoming delightfully visible through them. They are no longer vessels for the one true God. So may we all avoid laziness, and may we be diligent with the gifts God has given us so that we can portray an accurate and glorious picture of Him.

# God, where are You leading me today?

*April 22*

# Seeking the Blessing

*See to it that no one misses the grace of God and that no bitter root grows up to cause trouble and defile many. See that no one is sexually immoral, or is godless like Esau, who for a single meal sold his inheritance rights as the oldest son. Afterward, as you know, when he wanted to inherit this blessing, he was rejected. He could bring about no change of mind, though he sought the blessing with tears.* —Hebrews 12:15–17

God is so full of love. His heart beats for you . . . longs for you . . . waits for you . . . and desires to forgive you for foolishly falling for another love on this earth. Just do not play around with and abuse His loving invitation. Esau did not fully appreciate the blessing he had been given. When it came to choosing between his blessing and a bowl of stew, Esau went for the meal. His blessing had been a once-in-a-lifetime opportunity, and he gave it up for food. Does this sound familiar?

God has given each of us a wonderful opportunity—a chance to love Him and serve Him as our one true God. We should take this invitation very seriously, for it is offered with love and grace and mercy. We should seek His blessing and treasure it, and we should be mindful to never trade it in for some temporary earthly pleasure. Accept the invitation!

*The Spirit and the bride say, "Come!" And let him who hears say, "Come!" Whoever is thirsty, let him come; and whoever wishes, let him take the free gift of the water of life.* —Revelation 22:17

*April 23*

# God, where are You leading me today?

_April 24_

# Passing Down Our Idols

*"You shall not make for yourself an idol in the form of anything in heaven above or on the earth beneath or in the waters below. You shall not bow down to them or worship them; for I, the LORD your God, am a jealous God, punishing the children for the sin of the fathers to the third and fourth generation of those who hate me, but showing love to a thousand generations of those who love me and keep my commandments."* ⟶Exodus 20:4–6

We pass down our idols to our children, even through the fourth generation. This includes our false idol of food. In fact, America's children have never been so large, and everyone keeps blaming it on sedentary lifestyles and fast food. But you and I know the true reason—the reason that reaches down into the hearts of our children. We have *passed down* what we adore—the food—to the next generation. But the good news is that the solution is simple! Change what *you* adore, and your children will change what *they* adore. If you want to pass down the very best idol to your children, concentrate on devoting your own heart to the Father, and He will take care of the rest.

*April 25*

# God, where are You leading me today?

April 26

# God Disciplines His Children

*"My son, do not make light of the Lord's discipline, and do not lose heart when he rebukes you, because the Lord disciplines those he loves, and he punishes everyone he accepts as a son."* ━Hebrews 12:5b–6

As you are traveling through the hot desert of testing, think about this for a moment: Who invests more time in you than God? If you could only see the complete love of someone who takes the time to set up detailed testing, disciplining, and ways of escape just for you! What parent or teacher or friend has ever given you so much personal attention? Who else has ever spent so much time trying to guide you, teach you, and mold you according to His own heart? Who else has ever sent their Son to die for you? No one . . . only God loves you that much.

We should welcome testing, discipline, and even punishment, for it is a Father who loves His children who must punish them from time to time. So, my friends, do not despise it. You are a chosen son or daughter.

*April 27*

# God, where are You leading me today?

April 28

# Exercising Your Spiritual Muscles

*For physical training is of some value, but godliness has value for all things, holding promise for both the present life and the life to come.*

*—1 Timothy 4:8*

Physical exercise can be great for the body, but remember that training the heart in love and righteousness will help you right now *and* in eternity. You can strengthen your physical body here on earth, but you cannot take your physical body with you into heaven. However, if you strengthen your spiritual body—your heart, your mind, and your soul—that will be your key to entering heaven! Paul writes in First Timothy that physical training is of some value, but he also writes that we should train ourselves to be godly. So do not invest more time and energy in your physical muscles than you do in your spiritual muscles.

*April 29*

# God, where are You leading me today?

_____

_____

_____

_____

_____

_____

_____

_____

_____

_____

_____

_____

_____

_____

_____

_____

_____

_____

_____

_____

_____

_____

_____

_____

*April 30*

# You Can Be Done with Sin

*Therefore, since Christ suffered in his body, arm yourselves also with the same attitude, because he who has suffered in his body is done with sin. As a result, he does not live the rest of his earthly life for evil human desires, but rather for the will of God.* ━━1 Peter 4:1–2

Peter, who had failed Christ at one time, held the keys to the kingdom when he wrote the above words. Just as there were early skeptics who thought pioneer aviators could not overcome Earth's gravity, skeptics today do not believe that you can be done with sin, even though this scripture tells you that you can. The skeptics say that you are wasting your time, you are arrogant, and you are dreaming. When you do fall down, they gloat and mock, saying, "What is the matter? I thought you could overcome sin." Skeptics are inside *and* outside the church building; some of them even live with you. They say "once an alcoholic, always an alcoholic," or "once you become obese, you will just have to 'watch it' for the rest of your life."

Read Peter's statement again. Is this not one of the most exciting things you have ever read? I have broken free of the refrigerator's magnetism, and it no longer exerts a gravitational pull on me. I am flying, and you can too. Let's imitate the early pioneer pilots who reached their goals by setting their minds on what was *not* seen (their dreams of flying), rather than what *was* seen (their skeptics and the early, inevitable failures).

# God, where are You leading me today?

May 2

# God Shook the Earth

*"Obey these instructions as a lasting ordinance for you and your descendants. When you enter the land that the LORD will give you as he promised, observe this ceremony. And when your children ask you, 'What does this ceremony mean to you?' then tell them, 'It is the Passover sacrifice to the LORD, who passed over the houses of the Israelites in Egypt and spared our homes when he struck down the Egyptians.'" Then the people bowed down and worshiped. The Israelites did just what the LORD commanded Moses and Aaron.* ⟶*Exodus 12:24–28*

God made all of Egypt experience the terrifying plagues. Through the wind and the rain, lightning and hail, through a river of blood, insects and supernatural power, and even death itself, Satan and all the world saw that God and God alone was the one to worship, for He displayed superior power. He displayed His superior intellect, His appointment as the God of creation and as the King of kings, and His rightful position as the one true God of the universe. God commanded that this story be told from generation to generation because the message is foundational. God is indeed alive and is indeed the magnificent force creating and controlling the elements of the earth. He shook the earth to release the hold that the world had on the heart of man. He showed all nations that He was more powerful than the earth and its hold. Mankind would never again have to worry whether the world of food and other secret loves has more power than the God of the universe. God indeed has all the power!

*May 3*

# God, where are You leading me today?

*May 4*

# Do Not Grow Weary

*Therefore, since we are surrounded by such a great cloud of witnesses, let us throw off everything that hinders and the sin that so easily entangles, and let us run with perseverance the race marked out for us. Let us fix our eyes on Jesus, the author and perfecter of our faith, who for the joy set before him endured the cross, scorning its shame, and sat down at the right hand of the throne of God. Consider him who endured such opposition from sinful men, so that you will not grow weary and lose heart. In your struggle against sin, you have not yet resisted to the point of shedding your blood.*

*━Hebrews 12:1–4*

When you get discouraged and feel all alone, practice this: Imagine a whole room filled with all the great men and women of faith. Think of everyone who has been passionate for God and would do anything to please Him! Fix your eyes on Jesus, who knew the joy that was to come and therefore endured terrible things to show the power of the Father. Why should we be discouraged or feel alone? The men and women of great faith did much more than we do and they were required to endure greater hardship because of their faith, yet they never took their eyes and their hearts from the Father. Their actions should put a smile on your face as you think about how much they loved God. Try today to see the joy that is to come, so that you will not grow weary and lose heart!

# God, where are You leading me today?

May 6

# The Fear of Man

*Fear of man will prove to be a snare, but whoever trusts in the LORD is kept safe.* —Proverbs 29:25

One problem I have seen frequently that I believe is grievous to the Father is that we fear our family's rejection more than His. We put other people (our family members) above God in our hearts, and it shows. Where are the Abrahams who would willingly put a knife up to Isaac after God requested it? Even Jesus could not get much support from His family as He carried out His ministry and the will of the Father. Why do we seek man's approval over our Father's approval? If you will just stop seeking this approval from other people and look to the Lord for approval instead, you will feel such a release! God will be able to see that He is truly the one whose opinion you most care about. Once He trusts in this and finds you worthy of Him, He just might give you the approval—and even the honor—you desire from your family members.

# God, where are You leading me today?

May 8

# Let Your Soul Yearn

*How lovely is your dwelling place, O LORD Almighty! My soul yearns, even faints, for the courts of the LORD; my heart and my flesh cry out for the living God.* ━*Psalm 84:1–2*

Make sure that your soul longs for God and not for your past and secret loves. Do you remember all the loving concern and attention that you used to give to food? Can you recall how your heart used to long for all those foods that were forbidden on your latest diet? Do you remember how your heart and flesh seemed to cry out to be healthy and to be rid of the excess weight? Now, give *all* of this to God. Give your attention and concern to God and to His kingdom and His children. Let Him be the one you truly love, and let your soul long for His approval. Respond as your heart and flesh cry out for His perfect guidance and for the contentment that comes from obedience. The Lord's dwelling place has so much more to offer than the pantry! May your flesh cry out for the living God and not for the stupid food.

# God, where are You leading me today?

_May 10_

# Experiencing "Just Enough"

*The rabble with them began to crave other food, and again the Israelites started wailing and said, "If only we had meat to eat! We remember the fish we ate in Egypt at no cost—also the cucumbers, melons, leeks, onions and garlic. But now we have lost our appetite; we never see anything but this manna!" Moses heard the people of every family wailing, each at the entrance to his tent. The LORD became exceedingly angry, and Moses was troubled.* ⁓Numbers 11:4–6,10

I would like to take a moment and point out that God's manna diet did not include all the food groups—it was just a diet of bread provided by heaven. Yes, God gave them just bread and water to live on. A portion of the desert journey is learning the definition of "just enough" so that you can see how little it takes to live. How can you appreciate extra if you do not know the definition of enough? Some of you have never allowed your bodies to experience "just enough." You are always gathering more manna than you need. God got very angry at his children for trying to stop His decision for them to experience "just enough." We need to experience "just enough" financially, relationally, physiologically, and spiritually. Sometimes, even His involvement or His relationship with us is "just enough" so that we can appreciate a deeper relationship with Him. Once you develop it, you will then cherish it and care for it and nurture it with all your heart. A relationship with God is *everything*. Guard it with your life!

*May 11*

# God, where are You leading me today?

May 12

# Rush Toward the Giant

*David said to the Philistine, "You come against me with sword and spear and javelin, but I come against you in the name of the LORD Almighty, the God of the armies of Israel, whom you have defied. This day the LORD will hand you over to me, and I'll strike you down and cut off your head. Today I will give the carcasses of the Philistine army to the birds of the air and the beasts of the earth, and the whole world will know that there is a God in Israel. All those gathered here will know that it is not by sword or spear that the LORD saves; for the battle is the LORD's, and he will give all of you into our hands." As the Philistine moved closer to attack him, David ran quickly toward the battle line to meet him.* ━1 Samuel 17:45–48

The boy David defied anyone who was opposed to God, including a giant Philistine who struck fear in all those who faced him. In his lifetime, David would take stones, slings, and swords against more than a few people who were antagonistic toward the One whom he rightly knew was the glorious and perfect King of the universe. Even though David was a very successful warrior for the Lord, he made sure that all witnesses knew that every battle victory was the Lord's. David used the strength God gave him and he always gave praise to the Father, humbled before the power of the Lord. Today, prepare your stones and sling and rush toward the giant, and watch how the enemies of God will fall before His power.

*May 13*

# God, where are You leading me today?

May 14

# Searching for the Heart of God

*Oh, how I love your law! I meditate on it all day long. Your commands make me wiser than my enemies, for they are ever with me. I have more insight than all my teachers, for I meditate on your statutes. I have more understanding than the elders, for I obey your precepts. I call out to you; save me and I will keep your statutes. I rise before dawn and cry for help; I have put my hope in your word. My eyes stay open through the watches of the night, that I may meditate on your promises.* ➻Psalm 119:97–100,146–148

We have all traveled on a long spiritual journey—parallel to that of the Israelites—to get to the point where we are. We have had an exodus from our slavery and strongholds. By now, we have tasted the heavy testing of the desert, and we have either gotten the idea or we are stuck up to our necks in some sandpit. This desert is no ordinary testing. It is very heavy . . . and I know your pain. God gives us only what we can bear, and He knows the pain. The desert has been so hard for me, but I feel as if I am past the heavy testing. If I had to give you one piece of advice from my suffering, I would tell you this: Hang on to the Word of God. I am afraid to let the Bible get far from my side. Oh, the hours I have spent searching for the heart of God, sneaking into it like it was a box of chocolates, or opening it like it was a bank vault with a million dollars in it. My heart gets excited at the chance to sit down and see what the Father is going to tell me.

# God, where are You leading me today?

May 16

# The Depth of God's Pain

*Oh, the depth of the riches of the wisdom and knowledge of God! How unsearchable his judgments, and his paths beyond tracing out!*
*—Romans 11:33*

*The LORD was grieved that he had made man on the earth, and his heart was filled with pain.* *—Genesis 6:6*

Everything about God reaches far beyond what we are capable of understanding. His wisdom, His knowledge, His decisions, His actions, His heart, His love ... we just cannot comprehend the depth of God's character. Have you ever thought about how big God's heart is? His heart is large enough to love every person on earth as His child. But the sad thing is that the bigger the heart of love, the greater the pain when that love is rejected. We have caused Him that kind of pain, for we reject His love daily. In fact, we have caused Him so *much* pain that He has become angry with us, even to the point that He grieved over creating us, just as it says in Genesis 6:6 above. We are blessed, though, by God's grace and mercy. If we just turn around now and give Him all of our love and devotion, He will forgive us for the pain we have caused, and His arms will take us in.

# God, where are You leading me today?

*May 18*

# Everything Proclaims His Glory

*The heavens declare the glory of God; the skies proclaim the work of his hands. Day after day they pour forth speech; night after night they display knowledge. There is no speech or language where their voice is not heard. Their voice goes out into all the earth, their words to the ends of the world. In the heavens he has pitched a tent for the sun.* —Psalm 19:1–4

God speaks to us first one way and then another, the book of Job says. I can learn something about God in everything that is made: our voices, our language, everything. Even "man-made" objects are actually the work of God's hand, and everything that has been invented or created or discovered proclaims His glory. His personality is even clear to me in music. When someone plays an instrument, I only see God, both in the creation of the instrument and in the talent of the performer. God can sing from bass to soprano, and He is a virtuoso on any instrument. The personality of God is very clear to me now, and there is still so much more to learn!

*May 19*

# God, where are You leading me today?

May 20

# Passion for God

*As the deer pants for streams of water, so my soul pants for you, O God.*
　　　　　　　　　　　　　　　　　　　　*⸺Psalm 42:1*

You may feel that you are not emotional toward any-thing at all or that you don't have the passion that King David had for God. But think about this in the area of food. If I were to lock you up in a room that had no food in it, you might start off asking politely for something to eat. A while later, you would ask a little more forcefully. As time went on, you might resort to begging and bribing. Eventually you would be threatening, yelling, and scream-ing at me to let you out or to bring some food in. Some people might even threaten my life if I didn't get them some food. How many of you have broken into a buffet line or jumped out of the car to get ahead of the next group of people going into the same restaurant? I have even known of grown men who stole money from their children's piggy banks in order to sneak away and feed their own obsessive greed for food.

So now, have you been passionate about food? Probably so. This is true for any stronghold. So, you are emotional after all—and this is as it should be. Now transfer this emo-tion and passion over to God.

# God, where are You leading me today?

May 22

# Wisdom from Above

*Who is wise and understanding among you? Let him show it by his good life, by deeds done in the humility that comes from wisdom. But if you harbor bitter envy and selfish ambition in your hearts, do not boast about it or deny the truth. Such "wisdom" does not come down from heaven but is earthly, unspiritual, of the devil.* —*James 3:13–15*

Never blame God or Satan when you fall into temptation. The book of James sets the record straight. We are tempted by our very own evil desire, by bitter envy and selfish ambition in our hearts. If we truly trusted God, would we ever have envy or selfish ambition in our hearts? Of course not. As James states, we would be humble, wise, and understanding, and our lives would show it. Ask God to unveil any selfish ambition in your own heart, and ask Him to help you let go of it before it leads you to sin. Keep your heart and mind focused on God, and let Him take care of your life. That is wisdom from above.

# God, where are You leading me today?

May 24

# Are You Busy, or Merely a Busybody?

*In the name of the Lord Jesus Christ, we command you, brothers, to keep away from every brother who is idle and does not live according to the teaching you received from us. For you yourselves know how you ought to follow our example. We were not idle when we were with you, nor did we eat anyone's food without paying for it. On the contrary, we worked night and day, laboring and toiling so that we would not be a burden to any of you. We did this, not because we do not have the right to such help, but in order to make ourselves a model for you to follow. For even when we were with you, we gave you this rule: "If a man will not work, he shall not eat." We hear that some among you are idle. They are not busy; they are busybodies. Such people we command and urge in the Lord Jesus Christ to settle down and earn the bread they eat. And as for you, brothers, never tire of doing what is right.* ━2 Thessalonians 3:6–13*

Time is a precious commodity. It is strange how we always want more of it, and yet I have seen too much idle time result in nothing but trouble. Now, people with too much time on their hands may look busy, but they are not really busy—they are busybodies pumping people for information and getting too involved in the lives of other people. These people should be going to God for information instead of going to the sidewalk to gather the latest gossip. And if God doesn't give the information they are curious about, then it is none of their concern to start with. They should instead be spending their idle time working . . . working to earn their bread and working to further God's kingdom. The Bible says to stay away from every brother who is idle!

# God, where are You leading me today?

May 26

# Seeking Him for Who He Is

*He had no beauty or majesty to attract us to him, nothing in his appearance that we should desire him.*
—Isaiah 53:2b

*Therefore we do not lose heart. Though outwardly we are wasting away, yet inwardly we are being renewed day by day. For our light and momentary troubles are achieving for us an eternal glory that far outweighs them all. So we fix our eyes not on what is seen, but on what is unseen. For what is seen is temporary, but what is unseen is eternal.*
—2 Corinthians 4:16–18

When you are more interested in losing weight than getting close to God, you will really struggle in your desert walk. The basic obstacle here is a lack of faith. God has programmed you with the desire to lose weight, but if you want the reward of God (the weight loss) without really having to *deal* with God (obedience), then that is comparable to marrying someone for their money or their looks instead of for their heart and love. It is completely self-serving. If you knew God better, you would understand that He would give you everything you want if you would just truly seek Him for who He is instead of for what He can give you. This is the age-old love problem. God has tried to eliminate that problem by remaining invisible and sending His Son to earth in a manger, even giving Him an undesirable physical appearance. What we need to do is experience enough of His personality and ability that we fall in love with *Him,* and not with His things. Love Him and you will naturally lose the weight—not the other way around!

# God, where are You leading me today?

May 28

# Set Apart

*So he [Moses] stood at the entrance to the camp and said, "Whoever is for the LORD, come to me." And all the Levites rallied to him. Then he said to them, "This is what the LORD, the God of Israel, says: 'Each man strap a sword to his side. Go back and forth through the camp from one end to the other, each killing his brother and friend and neighbor.'" The Levites did as Moses commanded, and that day about three thousand of the people died. Then Moses said, "You have been set apart to the LORD today, for you were against your own sons and brothers, and he has blessed you this day."*
*⟢Exodus 32:26–29*

The Levites were set apart from that day forward to work in the house of the Lord because they showed that they loved God more than their own families. Once again, God had found people who had the heart of Abraham, who would hold a knife up to his very own Isaac.

A great purging of drastic measure took place that day in order to get through to the remaining living souls. A remnant of wholly devoted souls rose to the top that day. There was hope. A heart that could house a spirit of love, healthy fear, and trust for the Father was found in the Levites. And they would be the ones who would take care of the house of the Lord from that day forward.

*May 29*

# God, where are You leading me today?

*May 30*

# Just Say "No" to Your Strongholds

*For the grace of God that brings salvation has appeared to all men. It teaches us to say "No" to ungodliness and worldly passions, and to live self-controlled, upright and godly lives in this present age, while we wait for the blessed hope—the glorious appearing of our great God and Savior, Jesus Christ.* ━Titus 2:11–13

Are we living self-controlled, upright, and godly lives today? Sadly, there are too many of us who are not. We are saying "Yes" to ungodliness and worldly passions. We might find it easy to say "No" to some things, like murder or theft, but when it comes to the everyday things that tempt us, like extra food or the praise of men, we say "Well . . . maybe," or even "Yes!" But read the above passage again. It does not state that the grace of God teaches us to turn down a *little* ungodliness or *some* worldly passions. No . . . we must strive to be as self-controlled and upright as possible, and this means that we must say "No" to our strongholds today!

# God, where are You leading me today?

June 1

# Let God Fill Your Heart

*You have filled my heart with greater joy than when their grain and new wine abound.* ━*Psalm 4:7*

Sin is simply a misplaced heart. God weighs the motives of the heart and He knows what fills your heart. There is nothing wrong with things on earth, but if you *worship* these things, you will feel drained, lethargic, worn out, and emotionless. You will not have the energy to love your spouse, children, or friends. Your heart will remain empty because you never obtain what you are seeking.

God will never let your false gods fill you up. However, people continue to try; they have put their hearts into football and basketball, computers and cars, clothes and social climbing, chocolate and desserts, children and careers. Name it, and it can be adored to a fault—to a point of worship. But if you throw yourself into worshiping God, then He will guide your actions. They will not be draining, but rewarding. Your energy level will rise. Your heart will be filled with great joy—so much better than false idols could ever do.

# God, where are You leading me today?

June 3

# "I Love the Father"

*But the world must learn that I love the Father and that I do exactly what my Father has commanded me.* —*John 14:31a*

The Bible is full of stories about people who based their lives on having a passion for God: Noah, Abraham, Moses, David, John the Baptist, Jesus. We must learn from all of these people that God set before us . . . and especially from Jesus. All of these people have one thing in common—they love God above all things. They trust in God's judgment and guidance. They are wholehearted and passionate, and they love doing anything that God wants, because He is their Hero! Each of us should love the Father in the same way. When we do, serving Him is a pleasure and a privilege. Jesus said that He *loved* the Father, and He would do anything the Father asked. What a passion!

*June 4*

# God, where are You leading me today?

June 5

# Have Faith in God's Love

*Observe the commands of the LORD your God, walking in his ways and revering him. For the LORD your God is bringing you into a good land—a land with streams and pools of water, with springs flowing in the valleys and hills; a land with wheat and barley, vines and fig trees, pomegranates, olive oil and honey; a land where bread will not be scarce and you will lack nothing; a land where the rocks are iron and you can dig copper out of the hills.* —Deuteronomy 8:6–9

*In everything that he undertook in the service of God's temple and in obedience to the law and the commands, he sought his God and worked wholeheartedly. And so he prospered.* —2 Chronicles 31:21

Those who seek and obey God can expect to be blessed and to prosper. There is nothing more fun in life than looking for the attention and personal love of the Father. There are so many ways that He shows us His love every day. Because I have faith in His love for me, it is my desire to seek His will for my life, because I know He will take care of me. I love to do something His way and imagine that He is winking back at me. Spend each day looking for evidence of His love for you. Look for His heart and His personality in everything, and you will be rewarded. Every year with God, my life gets fuller and fuller—way beyond what I deserve. Sometimes I feel like my heart will burst with happiness!

*June 6*

# God, where are You leading me today?

June 7

# His Mighty Rescue

*Now the length of time the Israelite people lived in Egypt was 430 years. At the end of the 430 years, to the very day, all the LORD's divisions left Egypt. Because the LORD kept vigil that night to bring them out of Egypt, on this night all the Israelites are to keep vigil to honor the LORD for the generations to come.* ⟶*Exodus 12:40–42*

If you study the plagues, you will see that they are really just battles between God and Egypt—battles for our hearts. We learn from the plagues that even though God has made Himself invisible, analogous to tying His right hand behind His back in a fight, He was still able to definitively beat the competition to an unrecognizable pulp. God has done *His* homework. He has shown us His passionate, jealous love, and He has shown us that He is not going to sit still and let the competition steal our hearts away. God has shown us that He is going to rescue and save us, and that He will make a distinction between those who have a heart for Him and those who have a heart for Egypt. God's awesome massacre showed that He was the God of all gods. The Israelites' hearts were drawn to follow this mighty Warrior to the desert, and ours should, too! We should follow Him and give Him honor for all generations.

*June 8*

# God, where are You leading me today?

June 9

# God Can Fill
# Your Empty Heart

*"Hear, O my people, and I will warn you—if you would but listen to me, O Israel! You shall have no foreign god among you; shall not bow down to an alien god. I am the LORD your God, who brought you up out of Egypt. Open wide your mouth and I will fill it."* ⟶*Psalm 81:8–10*

We should no longer use chocolate cake to fill an empty heart! Psalm 81 tells us, "Open wide your mouth and I will fill it!" Open your heart to God and let Him fill you up, and this feeling you are searching for will be perfectly fulfilled. That chocolate cake will never give back to you— it only takes. But God always gives back! So the next time you are tempted to pick up that fork to fill your empty heart, go to God, ask for help, and ask Him to fill you up better than the world can. I have found out that He loves the challenge, and He loves to show off! After all, He has so much to give. Your job is to open wide your heart—let your pride go and open wide your heart. You are *not* to fill it. *His* job is to *fill* it!

# God, where are You leading me today?

# The Humble Are Exalted

*"Two men went up to the temple to pray, one a Pharisee and the other a tax collector. The Pharisee stood up and prayed about himself: 'God, I thank you that I am not like other men—robbers, evildoers, adulterers—or even like this tax collector. I fast twice a week and give a tenth of all I get.' But the tax collector stood at a distance. He would not even look up to heaven, but beat his breast and said, 'God, have mercy on me, a sinner.' I tell you that this man, rather than the other, went home justified before God. For everyone who exalts himself will be humbled, and he who humbles himself will be exalted."*  —Luke 18:10–14

In this parable, Jesus said that it was the humble tax collector who went home justified before God, and He said that everyone who humbles himself will be exalted, but those who exalt themselves will be humbled. With whom do you identify—the tax collector or the Pharisee? There is something foundational about the truth of who you are and who God is. The Pharisee was wrong about both. There is nothing more irritating than a prideful person, because that person just doesn't get it. The prideful person does not see that God is everything and what He says *goes*; He is the boss. The Pharisee was self-righteous. In other words, he made the rules and he met his own rules— he was "self-right." It is like creating your own school and awarding yourself a Ph.D. It is so *absurd!* We need to find God's words or suggestions, then meet those and tremble at His leading. That is true righteousness. There's a big difference—as far apart as the tax collector and the Pharisee.

*"This is the one I esteem: he who is humble and contrite in spirit, and trembles at my word."*  —Isaiah 66:2b

# God, where are You leading me today?

June 13

# Free to Love God

*Then the LORD said to Moses, "Stretch out your hand over the sea so that the waters may flow back over the Egyptians and their chariots and horsemen." Moses stretched out his hand over the sea, and at daybreak the sea went back to its place. The Egyptians were fleeing toward it, and the LORD swept them into the sea. The water flowed back and covered the chariots and horsemen—the entire army of Pharaoh that had followed the Israelites into the sea. Not one of them survived.* ▬Exodus 14:26–28

After the Israelites passed to the other side of the Red Sea by God's mighty hand, there was much singing and dancing. The Egyptians who pursued the Israelites were found lying dead on the seashore. God no longer allowed the Egyptians to have control over His beloved children. In the same way, food or any other stronghold no longer has control over you. Look at the ruins of Egypt. That civilization has been cursed and has never returned to its former glory as a world power. It is only the lies of Satan that make you think that a pan of brownies still has control over you. The truth is that you do not have to obey food anymore—you are free to love God and obey Him! I truly believe that we are the most blessed beings alive today to be able to get this chance to be devoted to God.

# God, where are You leading me today?

# No Secret Agendas

by *Michael Shamblin*

*"I the LORD search the heart and examine the mind."* ➼ *Jeremiah 17:10a*

Do not think that you can conceal your hidden motives and secret agendas from God. Trying to hide your heart from God is impossible! He created us, inside and outside, and He searches our hearts and our minds. He is the only One who truly knows *who* and *what* we are deep down. Do not try to hide your thoughts from the Lord, but rather, freely share your thoughts, desires, and agendas with Him. Instead of thinking that you can fool the Almighty God, try to please Him by asking Him to lead your thoughts and by doing His will. Give your heart to the Father, and watch what He can do in your life!

*June 16*

# God, where are You leading me today?

June 17

# What Does God's Face Look Like?

*One thing I ask of the LORD, this is what I seek: that I may dwell in the house of the LORD all the days of my life, to gaze upon the beauty of the LORD and to seek him in his temple. For in the day of trouble he will keep me safe in his dwelling; he will hide me in the shelter of his tabernacle and set me high upon a rock. Then my head will be exalted above the enemies who surround me; at his tabernacle will I sacrifice with shouts of joy; I will sing and make music to the LORD. Hear my voice when I call, O LORD; be merciful to me and answer me. My heart says of you, "Seek his face!" Your face, LORD, I will seek.* —Psalm 27:4–8

God will hear your music and your shouts of joy if you seek His face with all your heart. This means that you must seek God's face in everything you do. You need to see if He is smiling at what you are doing or if He is frowning at what you are thinking or doing. Remember that God sees *inside* our hearts and our minds. He will have an opinion about everything we consider. We should always look to Him with all our thoughts to seek His guidance first. Sometimes, when I know God sees the love for Him I have in my heart, or when I know He hears me defending His kingdom, I feel like I can see God winking at me. I really do believe God danced the day I was born, just like He danced the day *you* were born. Seek His face, because that is all that matters! If you have lived for the Lord, you know the face you will finally see will have a smile on it . . . and your heart will melt.

# God, where are You leading me today?

# How to Put Strongholds on the Back Burner

*"Return, faithless Israel," declares the* LORD, *"I will frown on you no longer, for I am merciful," declares the* LORD, *"I will not be angry forever. Only acknowledge your guilt—you have rebelled against the* LORD *your God, you have scattered your favors to foreign gods under every spreading tree, and have not obeyed me," declares the* LORD. *"Return, faithless people," declares the* LORD, *"for I am your husband."*          ⟞Jeremiah 3:12b–14a

Be assured that you *can* return to God or transfer your love to God. Even if you have developed a heart-pounding crush on food—you dress for the food in your stretch clothes, you plan secret rendezvous with the food late at night, you hear the voice of the one you love, and thinking about food is even what gets you out of bed in the morning—moving from Egypt to the desert is as easy as when you had a crush on some guy or girl in high school. You *loved* that person, but when the *new* guy or girl walked in, you didn't even want the old one to call your name. You didn't want him to write you notes or phone you, and you even avoided walking down the hallway that his locker was on.

The old lover became repulsive—and that's how it is with food for me now. I don't want my old love, food, to call my name unless I'm hungry. The good news is that your heart was made to turn around and return to God, and the simple tool to do this is called "choice." If I ever feel my heart beginning to wander, I find something God has made, like flowers, and I marvel at Him all over again. When you choose today whom you will serve—our awesome Father—and focus on Him, your heart will follow. It's automatic. And you will find your heart and mind back on the Father, where they belong.

*June 20*

# God, where are You leading me today?

# Setting Our Hearts

*Since, then, you have been raised with Christ, set your hearts on things above, where Christ is seated at the right hand of God. Set your minds on things above, not on earthly things. For you died, and your life is now hidden with Christ in God. When Christ, who is your life, appears, then you also will appear with him in glory.* ━Colossians 3:1–4

Listen to that again: Set your hearts and minds on things above, where Christ is seated. You know, we set a lot of things in our life. Think about it. We set our alarm clocks, and we set the timers on our ovens. We set the radio, and we set the television for our favorite channel. We mark our paths to work, and we set the dates for our vacations. We set our VCRs to tape when we are gone, and we set our coffee pots to brew coffee before we wake up.

Yes, we spend a lot of our time and energy setting things. But how much time and energy do we spend setting our hearts and our minds on Jesus Christ, our very best advocate to the Father and the One who has saved us from sin? Today, let the oven timer and VCR and radio wait. Before you set anything else, set your heart and your mind on things above.

# God, where are You leading me today?

June 23

# The Cloud and the Sea

*For I do not want you to be ignorant of the fact, brothers, that our forefathers were all under the cloud and that they all passed through the sea. They were all baptized into Moses in the cloud and in the sea. They all ate the same spiritual food and drank the same spiritual drink; for they drank from the spiritual rock that accompanied them, and that rock was Christ.*
*—1 Corinthians 10:1–4*

The cloud of God represented the presence of God. They were all baptized in this cloud and into Moses and the sea, or in other words, surrounded, covered, consecrated, and dedicated to God with the same goals and directions at the outset of this desert journey. Most of you have the goals of the Father at the outset of *your* desert journey, also. You have been baptized into the following of Jesus Christ, and you have realized that the only water of life available in the desert is from Him. Continue to surround yourself with Jesus Christ, and you will live and blossom in the hot desert of testing. If you are baptized, the water is in your ears, nose, eyes, and all around you. Do the same with the will of the Father.

*June 24*

# God, where are You leading me today?

# He Calls Us Friends

*"My command is this: Love each other as I have loved you. Greater love has no one than this, that he lay down his life for his friends. You are my friends if you do what I command. I no longer call you servants, because a servant does not know his master's business. Instead, I have called you friends, for everything that I learned from my Father I have made known to you. You did not choose me, but I chose you and appointed you to go and bear fruit— fruit that will last. Then the Father will give you whatever you ask in my name."* —John 15:12–16

Jesus calls us His friends. He loves us, He will lay down His life for us, and He shares with us everything He has learned from God. All He asks of us is that if we are His friends, we will obey what He commands. So what are His commands? First, to love Him with all our heart, soul, mind, and strength. Then, to love our neighbor as ourselves. Does this sound like we are going in circles? It kind of does at times. It looks as if the genuine article—the heart that truly does love God—will, at the same time, be obedient by loving God and others. So Jesus was saying, "If you love Me, it will show." Love and obedience walk hand in hand; in fact, you will love obeying God's commands. Think about it this way: Does a person who loves football say, "Oh, another football game is on TV. I guess I *have* to watch it . . . ?" No! They plan for it and look forward to it and invite others to watch it with them. They *savor* it. That's the relationship you will have—a relationship where you love and the object of your affection loves you back!

*June 26*

# God, where are You leading me today?

# Obedience = Freedom, Disobedience = Slavery

*Again the Israelites did evil in the eyes of the LORD. They served the Baals and the Ashtoreths, and the gods of Aram, the gods of Sidon, the gods of Moab, the gods of the Ammonites and the gods of the Philistines. And because the Israelites forsook the LORD and no longer served him, he became angry with them. He sold them into the hands of the Philistines and the Ammonites, who that year shattered and crushed them. For eighteen years they oppressed all the Israelites on the east side of the Jordan in Gilead, the land of the Amorites.*　　　　　　　　　　　　　　　　　——Judges 10:6–8

The reason someone would want to return to the slavery of dieting is because of disobedience. However, they blame the freedom, saying, "Oh, there's too much freedom in Weigh Down. I'm bingeing because you say we can eat any food, and I'm not used to the freedom." Well, here is a major point—you cannot mix *freedom* and *disobedience*. Obedience and freedom go together, and disobedience and slavery go together. Over and over in the Old Testament, God would rescue the Israelites, they would again become idolatrous and disobedient, and then God would have to send them back into slavery until He thought they were ready to be obedient again. When they repented, God would take them back.

If you want freedom, you should strive to be completely obedient; if you are disobedient, turn immediately back to God in repentance. In other words, if you are obedient to stomach hunger and fullness, you are free to eat anything you are craving. Your focus is on obedience, and you are now free from judgment, free from fat, free from scales, free from weighing and measuring, free from calories, free from guilt, free to wear the clothes you want—you're free,

*June 28*

free, *free!* On the other hand, if you are disobedient to the amounts God is asking you to eat and the scales creep up, you will be forced into counting fat grams and watching the scales, all because you refuse to eat less food. The food you eat will have to be rabbit food again, and you will be enslaved once more.

God, where are You leading me today?

# Are You Willing to be Gathered?

*"O Jerusalem, Jerusalem, you who kill the prophets and stone those sent to you, how often I have longed to gather your children together, as a hen gathers her chicks under her wings, but you were not willing. Look, your house is left to you desolate. For I tell you, you will not see me again until you say, 'Blessed is he who comes in the name of the Lord'"* ——Matthew 23:37–39
*"But your hearts must be fully committed to the LORD our God, to live by his decrees and obey his commands, as at this time."* ——1 Kings 8:61

God so adamantly opposes the heart turning away from Him that He gives us many word pictures and biblical examples to teach us never to consider this action. In Matthew, we learn how God longs to gather us to Himself, where He can protect us and provide for us. And yet we continue to turn our backs, freely giving our hearts to things on this earth that cannot protect us or give us anything in return. How insulting this must be to God! We must give our *whole* hearts to God—not just divided hearts. First Kings tells us that our hearts must be *fully* committed. It does not say that we can merely think about God every now and then. Let's learn from and remember all the examples and lessons God gives us in the Bible, and start today giving everything we can to Him and keeping our hearts focused on Him alone.

# God, where are You leading me today?

_____

_____

_____

_____

_____

_____

_____

_____

_____

_____

_____

_____

_____

_____

_____

_____

_____

_____

_____

_____

_____

_____

_____

_____

_____

*July 1*

# Do You Worry about God's House?

*Moses was faithful as a servant in all God's house, testifying to what would be said in the future. But Christ is faithful as a son over God's house. And we are his house, if we hold on to our courage and the hope of which we boast.* ━━Hebrews 3:5–6

Our prayer should be so natural. In fact, I talk to God all day long. Until now, we have been very attentive to our stronghold, but now we need to reverse this. A wonderful way to direct our hearts to God is to see things from God's perspective. Have empathy for His purpose, His will, His goals. Are you concerned about how clean or decorated your own house is? Well, what about His house? Think about all the hearts that need to be cleaned up. Are you concerned about your business? Then take time to think about His business. He has a hard time finding any devoted employees. Worrying more about God's children than your own children is the faith that God is looking for. Are you concerned about someone's pregnancy or miscarriage? How about all the miscarriages that God has experienced with hearts that never beat for Him?

When I pray, my prayers reflect more interest and concern for Him than for myself; as a result, I've seen God come in and take care of my house, my business, and my children. This book is not large enough to hold the blessings that I have received because the zeal of His house consumes me. Work on this attitude, and you will fall in love with God.

# God, where are You leading me today?

July 3

# Develop Your Spiritual Senses

*The LORD reigns, let the earth be glad; let the distant shores rejoice. Clouds and thick darkness surround him; righteousness and justice are the foundation of his throne. Fire goes before him and consumes his foes on every side. His lightning lights up the world; the earth sees and trembles. The mountains melt like wax before the LORD, before the Lord of all the earth. The heavens proclaim his righteousness, and all the peoples see his glory.*
*—Psalm 97:1–6*

There are many people who love other people and have devoted their lives to mankind but do not love God. God knows that He is invisible and that we cannot get the usual gratification of actually hearing, touching, smelling, tasting, and seeing Him. If we did, we would all automatically fall down and worship Him, since He is the best looking and most coordinated and the smartest—far above man and all false gods.

So to keep your focus and to keep your priorities on God first and on man second, develop your *spiritual* sight, hearing, smell, taste, and touch. Once you develop these and you taste and see that God is a genius, your physical senses will take a back seat and your spiritual senses will take the front driver's seat!

*July 4*

# God, where are You leading me today?

July 5

# The State of the Church

*One of the seven angels who had the seven bowls full of the seven last plagues came and said to me, "Come, I will show you the bride, the wife of the Lamb."*
*—Revelation 21:9*
*The Spirit and the bride say, "Come!" And let him who hears say, "Come!" Whoever is thirsty, let him come; and whoever wishes, let him take the free gift of the water of life.* *—Revelation 22:17*

I hear many people claim that their six-to-twelve-month plateau in weight loss is the desert. But think with me. If we call this a desert, then it is quicksand. And now we're worse off than we were before, because we've labeled this delusion as a more progressive part of the journey of salvation instead of a retreat. Instead of depicting the desert as a wonderful place to grow nearer to God, we have concocted such a defeated desert scene that young sojourners would never want to follow in our footsteps.

I see this as the largest delusion of the body of Christ—an invisible, undetectable cancer that has permeated every denomination. Instead of a healthy, athletic, powerful, and magnetic body of Christ, we've made a sad, sickly, cancerous body of Christ lying on a hospital bed with an IV bag. We devise evangelical church programs to invite the world into this "saved" state, and yet we can't even get up and walk. This is hardly an evangelical state for the body of Christ. Who wants this? Week after week, people sit on the church pew, enslaved to the world. They claim, "I'm saved, I'm saved," and yet their necks are strangled by a ball and chain, and they wonder why they can't drink in the water of life and gain strength from the bread of life.

# God, where are You leading me today?

July 7

# The Fountain of Life

*But the LORD is the true God; he is the living God, the eternal King. When he is angry, the earth trembles; the nations cannot endure his wrath. "Tell them this: 'These gods, who did not make the heavens and the earth, will perish from the earth and from under the heavens.'"* ⟐ *Jeremiah 10:10–11*
*"My people have committed two sins: They have forsaken me, the spring of living water, and have dug their own cisterns, broken cisterns that cannot hold water."* ⟐ *Jeremiah 2:13*

Have we forgotten what a god is? A god—a true God—doesn't *need* anything. If He did, He wouldn't be a God. Jehovah doesn't need anything you could give Him in money or time or help. He doesn't need your heart or your soul or your mind. That's why He can give it back to you, plus some. He is the Source of time, and He is the Source of love. He is the Supplier of gold, and He is the Creator of food. He is the Fountain of life. Yes, I have experienced this truth. He is the *Alpha*, and He is the *Omega*. He is the Beginning, and He is the End. He is the *only* source—find me another. Try giving your heart to football, baseball, basketball, or hockey. As you adore the athletes, the irony is that many times you become a couch potato and somehow full of anger. Try making your spouse a god, and you will run them off. Your spouse is your helpmate, not your god. Just try giving your heart to money, and you'll find yourself in poverty. Try giving yourself to sexual lust, and you'll find yourself divorced, lonely, or diseased. Find me a god—you can't. There's only one. He is the *only* true fountain of life. Don't try digging your own wells.

# God, where are You leading me today?

July 9

# Seeking God First

*But seek [ye] first his kingdom and his righteousness, and all these things will be given to you as well.* —Matthew 6:33

Most of our desert storms break out because we do not automatically seek God *first* as we are told to do. Most of us have come only as close as "seek ye fifth" or "seek ye sixth," but "seek ye first" is not the natural instinct it should be. Instead of trying to do things or worrying about things that are not part of your job description, practice giving your worries to God. Spend your time worrying about His kingdom—starting with your own heart, then the hearts of His children. Worry about His house more than your house. Once this habit is formed, it will make a great difference in your weight loss and in every area of your life. God will come back in and do more for your children and your house than you could think or imagine.

*July 10*

# God, where are You leading me today?

# Be on Your Watch

*He told them this parable: "Look at the fig tree and all the trees. When they sprout leaves, you can see for yourselves and know that summer is near. Even so, when you see these things happening, you know that the kingdom of God is near. I tell you the truth, this generation will certainly not pass away until all these things have happened. Heaven and earth will pass away, but my words will never pass away. Be careful, or your hearts will be weighed down with dissipation, drunkenness and the anxieties of life, and that day will close on you unexpectedly like a trap. For it will come upon all those who live on the face of the whole earth. Be always on the watch, and pray that you may be able to escape all that is about to happen, and that you may be able to stand before the Son of Man."* ⸺Luke 21:29–36

Jesus spoke the above words as a precaution to us to stay awake. We must remain aware and focused on the kingdom of God and its advancement. If we continue to focus on the worries of everyday life, the day of the Lord will appear before we even realize what is happening, and it will be like being caught in a trap. In other words, if we focus on this earth, it will only weigh us down and keep us from looking up to God in heaven. Jesus tells us to be on the watch, and one day we will be able to stand before God without worry.

*July 12*

# God, where are You leading me today?

_July 13_

# Jesus Parts the Impossible Barrier

*Therefore, if anyone is in Christ, he is a new creation; the old has gone, the new has come! All this is from God, who reconciled us to himself through Christ and gave us the ministry of reconciliation: that God was reconciling the world to himself in Christ, not counting men's sins against them. And he has committed to us the message of reconciliation.*
*—2 Corinthians 5:17–19*

There is no way to get from Egypt to the desert unless you find a way to cross the Red Sea. The Red Sea is a big barrier. You cannot swim across it because the currents would wash you away. In the same way, there is no way we can gain the opportunity to get to the heart of the Father on our own. We live on the wrong side of the tracks. We are poor and He is rich. We are unholy and He is holy. We are imperfect and He is perfect, good-looking, omnipotent, intelligent, and powerful. But here is the great news— the sacrifice of Jesus parts this impossible barrier and allows us to walk on dry land to the heart of God, away from the slavery of strongholds. God has reconciled the world to Himself in Christ. Jesus is worthy of praise for bringing the two hearts together!

# God, where are You leading me today?

July 15

# The Small Request of God

*"The kingdom of God does not come with your careful observation, nor will people say, 'Here it is,' or 'There it is,' because the kingdom of God is within you."* ⬤～*Luke 17:20b–21*

We cannot love the food and enjoy God; we should be loving God and enjoying the food. When we seek God first, a relationship is birthed, but God pulls back from the heart of the one who chooses other gods to adore. How could we ever put God in second place? My friends, this cannot be. It's one thing to be caught red-handed one time with another lover, but many of us are *repeatedly* choosing to secretly embrace something else on this earth. We even bring it into the only place in the world that is not sup-posed to have the world in it—our place of worship, the only place on earth where God asks for it to be just Him.

You see, God has allowed the entire earth to be under the control of Satan. That's more than fair, don't you agree? Now, can't we allow just *one* sanctuary where God has our full attention without any competition for our heart? No, we've brought the world into the church and into our hearts. It is unbearable to think about how painful and how insulting this is to God, yet how entertaining this is to Satan. The kingdom of God is within your heart. Wor-ship Him, and lay the food and all the other idols down. Let's stop entertaining Satan at God's expense.

# God, where are You leading me today?

July 17

# Look for the Fruit

*Brothers, think of what you were when you were called. Not many of you were wise by human standards; not many were influential; not many were of noble birth. But God chose the foolish things of the world to shame the wise; God chose the weak things of the world to shame the strong. He chose the lowly things of this world and the despised things—and the things that are not—to nullify the things that are, so that no one may boast before him.*
*—1 Corinthians 1:26–29*

*But avoid foolish controversies and genealogies and arguments and quarrels about the law, because these are unprofitable and useless. Warn a divisive person once, and then warn him a second time. After that, have nothing to do with him. You may be sure that such a man is warped and sinful; he is self-condemned.*
*—Titus 3:9–11*

How can we know how to live? In today's world, people often turn to those who have met the world's standards of academic excellence for the answers about how to live from day to day. Other people turn to those who have achieved the world's standards of wealth or popularity for an example of how to live. And there are still others who do not want a simple answer, but want to have scholarly debates and arguments before settling upon answers to life's questions.

But what does the Bible say? The Bible states that we should stay away from debates and arguments, and that the wisdom of the world will be made foolish by our awesome God! It also tells us how to know who to follow—by looking for the fruits of the teaching. The blind receiving sight and the crippled receiving the ability to walk were evidences Jesus used to show that the Almighty God was behind what He was doing. This has always been the barometer in my life: If a principle is from God, it will bear fruit. It will give you peace that is virtually free of anger,

*July 18*

and it will liberate you from compulsive behaviors. You will ultimately feel a deep, loving nature permeating your soul, in contrast to an unloving nature at the root and base of your soul. So if you are looking for answers, listen to people who are focused on the Lord's will and who listen to God's Word, because He is simply and purely a Genius.

God, where are You leading me today?

# Love, Knowledge, and Obedience

*Remember the LORD your God led you all the way in the desert these forty years, to humble you and to test you in order to know what was in your heart, whether or not you would keep his commands.* ➥*Deuteronomy 8:2*
*"Whoever has my commands and obeys them, he is the one who loves me. He who loves me will be loved by my Father, and I too will love him and show myself to him."* ➥*John 14:21*
*We know that we have come to know him if we obey his commands. The man who says, "I know him," but does not do what he commands is a liar, and the truth is not in him. But if anyone obeys his word, God's love is truly made complete in him. This is how we know we are in him: Whoever claims to live in him must walk as Jesus did.* ➥*1 John 2:3–6*

From the context of the passage from Deuteronomy 8, it looks like obedience is a big factor in knowing what is truly in our hearts. This is backed up by the words spoken by Jesus in John 14 and First John 2. Jesus would try to make it as clear as possible, first saying it one way, then another. He was making sure that we got the message while He was down on earth. So obedience is an important way—if not the major way—to measure and grow the love in our heart for God. After all, it is how our children love us, trust us, and respect us, and obedience is how employers know the hearts of employees. Patronizing obedience and false love are eventually revealed. Spend your time and energy loving God and learning more about Him, and obedience will come naturally.

# God, where are You leading me today?

July 21

# Earnestly Seek Him

*"You may ask me for anything in my name, and I will do it."*
➤*John 14:14*

*And without faith it is impossible to please God, because anyone who comes to him must believe that he exists and that he rewards those who earnestly seek him.*
➤*Hebrews 11:6*

We fell in love with the food by giving it our heart, soul, mind, and strength. We obeyed it. It called us from the bed in the morning, and we used our strength to prepare it. We also used our strength to force more of it down into the body than the body called for. We gave it our mind all day long by looking through recipe books and discussing the latest diets with our friends, asking, "What do you get to eat on *your* diet?" We lusted after the foods that were on the menu, and we gave our hearts to the ten o'clock binge. To convert this love for the refrigerator to a love for God, we need to *obey* God and seek *Him*, not the food. Every time we obey God with regard to food or with anything He is putting on our heart to work on, we will fall more in love with Him. Note that we are to earnestly—which means with a true heart—seek *Him*, not His money or His power, but Him. And the reason we fall in love through obedience, or keeping His commands, is that He answers the prayers of those who obey Him, seek Him, and ask of Him.

# God, where are You leading me today?

July 23

# The God of All Comfort

*A bruised reed he will not break, and a smoldering wick he will not snuff out.*                    ━Isaiah 42:3a

Most people do not know how to comfort another human being. When my collie, Virginia, had puppies, it was so fun raising the little balls of fur. But I noticed that if one of them got left out of the feeding or got stuck between a table and chair or got turned around for a while, the other puppies didn't care. They just did not care about anything but their own personal needs. This is true in the animal world, and I have found it to be basically true for mankind, too. But God is totally different. As every child instinctively runs to his mother to show her his "hurt" so she can kiss it to make it better, we can always run to the Father to help our hurt go away. God will never be more concerned about His own needs than ours, and He will never turn away from us. When we come to Him for help, we will suddenly become the most important person to Him, and He will be there for us, no matter what time it is or what our need is.

# God, where are You leading me today?

# The Trainable Hearts of Children

*Train a child in the way he should go, and when he is old he will not turn from it.* ⟶*Proverbs 22:6*

Because the heart of a child is so trainable, it is important that we do not get in the way of God by teaching and suggesting things that confuse them. To teach children how to eat, you must first learn how to turn your child over to the Father. There are many books about how parents should raise their children, but I know better than to suggest that you are the "all in all" for your children. Rather, I suggest information about how to be wholly devoted to the Father, and then how to get your heart right so that you can experience what I have experienced—God being the personal tutor of your children. God's plan is uncomplicated. You do not have to be talented to be able to rejoice in having great children. It starts with *you* . . . you want to get your own heart right with food (or any stronghold), because we pass our idols down from one generation to the next generation.

# God, where are You leading me today?

July 27

# He Who Seeks, Finds

*O God, you are my God, earnestly I seek you; my soul thirsts for you, my body longs for you, in a dry and weary land where there is no water. I have seen you in the sanctuary and beheld your power and your glory. Because your love is better than life, my lips will glorify you. I will praise you as long as I live, and in your name I will lift up my hands. My soul will be satisfied as with the richest of foods; with singing lips my mouth will praise you.* —Psalm 63:1–5

You know, the thought and smell of food is what used to get me out of the bed in the morning years ago. Now, thinking about God and what kind of day He is planning for me is what gets me out of bed. All my senses are given over to God. I dress for Him. Although I do not see Him visibly, I can sense when He is near. I am hungry to read His Word. I ask Him to help me and guide me in everything, big and small, throughout the day. And I have found that since my senses have come alive to Him, I can recognize all the times that He answers my prayers in very personal and special ways. So many special little prayers were answered for one woman that she told me she does not even call things a "coincidence" anymore, but a "God-incidence!" Today, ask God to guide your day and pray for what you need from Him. Then, keep your senses alert and watch as He opens the door to you!

*July 28*

# God, where are You leading me today?

# The Lord's Gentle Whisper

*The LORD said, "Go out and stand on the mountain in the presence of the LORD, for the LORD is about to pass by." Then a great and powerful wind tore the mountains apart and shattered the rocks before the LORD, but the LORD was not in the wind. After the wind there was an earthquake, but the LORD was not in the earthquake. After the earthquake came a fire, but the LORD was not in the fire. And after the fire came a gentle whisper. When Elijah heard it, he pulled his cloak over his face and went out and stood at the mouth of the cave. Then a voice said to him, "What are you doing here, Elijah?"*　　　　　　　　　　　　　　　—1 Kings 19:11–13

This story about Elijah demonstrates that you need to watch for the Lord very carefully. He is such a gentleman—He will not push Himself on you, so you must listen closely for His gentle whisper. Elijah heard the Lord's whisper and obeyed it. We fell in love with food this way. We listened carefully to its whisper from the pantry. We heard its small voice calling us from the refrigerator late at night, and we obeyed it. Make sure today that you tell your old boss, food, that you do not have to do anything that it says! And then, make sure you only have eyes and ears for the Lord God Almighty. Listen for His whisper today.

_____

_____

_____

_____

_____

_____

_____

# God, where are You leading me today?

# The Beautiful Nights

*Sing for joy to God our strength; shout aloud to the God of Jacob! Begin the music, strike the tambourine, play the melodious harp and lyre. Sound the ram's horn at the New Moon, and when the moon is full, on the day of our Feast; this is a decree for Israel, an ordinance of the God of Jacob.*
*—Psalm 81:1–4*

Over the years, God has awakened me in the middle of the night to see the clear full moon. Every time I see it, I have so much appreciation in my heart for God's handiwork. I feel like God has been robbed, because full moons have often been associated with werewolves and the appearance of evil spirits. The truth is quite the opposite—these beautiful nights truly belong to the Lord! There are 18 references to New Moon and full moon celebrations among the Israelites. Today, we know that our hearts should be as devoted one day as the next, and we know that one day is not any more special than another. We should never neglect praising God for all the variety He provides to make Himself known and to make life fun and exciting! Let's put a stop on full moons being associated with werewolves. Let's return the full moon to the setting where it belongs—in praise of God!

*August 1*

# God, where are You leading me today?

August 2

# Are You Pure in Heart?

*Blessed are the pure in heart, for they will see God.* ━━Matthew 5:8

We learn in the Bible what type of heart will know God and see His kingdom. It is the trusting heart of a child who wants to be near Jesus. It is the faithful heart of Abraham placing Isaac on the altar. It is the strong and courageous heart of David stepping forward to face Goliath. It is the loving heart of Jesus suffering on the cross. It is the humble heart of the thief who hangs beside Him.

Jesus tells us in Matthew 5 what type of heart to strive for. A *pure* heart. A heart that is filled with love and trust and devotion to the Father. A heart that is not soiled by selfishness, greed, hate, or envy. A heart that is pure. You can be pure in heart, and you can see God. How? Well, look to Philippians 4:8: "Finally, brothers, whatever is true, whatever is noble, whatever is right, whatever is pure, whatever is lovely, whatever is admirable—if anything is excellent or praiseworthy—think about such things." In other words, empty your heart of things that are not pure and fill it with a strong focus on the Lord. Pray for Him to guide your heart and your spirit, and you will begin to see God in everything. "To the pure, all things are pure" (Titus 1:15a). To the impure, all things are impure.

*August 3*

# God, where are You leading me today?

August 4

# The Pursuit of the Father First

*For the message of the cross is foolishness to those who are perishing, but to us who are being saved it is the power of God. For it is written: "I will destroy the wisdom of the wise; the intelligence of the intelligent I will frustrate." Where is the wise man? Where is the scholar? Where is the philosopher of this age? Has not God made foolish the wisdom of the world? For since in the wisdom of God the world through its wisdom did not know him, God was pleased through the foolishness of what was preached to save those who believe.* ━1 Corinthians 1:18–21

Now, there is nothing wrong with pursuing academics to honor and glorify the Father, but if it were really and truly to glorify the Father, why would you be upset if you made a "B" on a report card? Well, you wouldn't. Being upset with teachers or with yourself or with anything only reveals that the glory is for *self*. Nothing is harder on a teacher than a parent and child team that is existing for the glory of the child. Nothing is harder on a coach than a parent/child combination that lives for the glory of the child.

These parents do not know the miraculous actuality of the "seek ye first," no-compromise lifestyle. Unfortunately, they encourage goals that only get the child more and more caught up in a rat race that will never satisfy. It is such an exploitation of the son or the daughter.

The mistaken belief is that this "seek ye first" lifestyle is an ungodly and unbalanced lifestyle. "Isn't it true," they argue, "that God wants you to have to make it in this life?" But this lack of understanding of God's personality and will is not going to save you or your child. In fact, God Himself says that His people perish from a lack of knowledge of Him (Hosea 4:6).

We learn from Matthew 6:33 that if you "seek first his kingdom and his righteousness," then "all these things will be given to you as well." Learning the true meaning of "seek ye first" will give you a harvest of blessings overflowing. In other words, you will save the child from the pain of loving this earth and the emptiness of a misguided mission if you teach the child to go first to the Father, expect all things from Him, and develop all gifts to His glory only.

# God, where are You leading me today?

# Love Others as Yourself

*After all, no one ever hated his own body, but he feeds and cares for it, just as Christ does the church—for we are members of his body.*

*—Ephesians 5:29–30*

The Bible tells us that we naturally love and care for ourselves. Since this is true, we should take the actions of love that we give ourselves and give them to someone else, too. As Jesus said in Leviticus 19:18, "Love your neighbor as yourself." Show concern for others—feed them, clothe them, and care for them. Do not focus constantly on pampering yourself, because it will only provide temporary delight, and you will despise your overly self-indulgent actions. It also turns other people off, making you even more isolated.

People of the world say that what you feel about yourself dictates whether you will have a good "eating" day. But I say getting your focus off self and onto God and obedience to Him will cause you to have a good "eating" day. If you love and trust the Lord, you will feed yourself the appropriate amount and not indulge in desire eating. You will be more in love with God for saving you from preoccupation with yourself. Since we do love ourselves, there should be a healthy, appropriate focus on care of self. But we tend to think if a little bit is good, then a lot is better. However, in the case of excessive self-love, it is empty and usually empties our pocketbooks. The balanced way leads to life; the other leads to death.

# God, where are You leading me today?

_August 8_

# His Favor Lasts a Lifetime

*Sing to the LORD, you saints of his; praise his holy name. For his anger lasts only a moment, but his favor lasts a lifetime; weeping may remain for a night, but rejoicing comes in the morning.* —Psalm 30:4–5

There have been so many times that I have sat in church on a Sunday evening and watched people listlessly drag themselves through the motions of their worship. These are the same people who will have a red and white pom-pom and apply red and white paint on their faces to root for their favorite college team. They jump up after the worship service—which is sometimes a sad name for what actually took place—and rush to basketball games for their true worship. They know the name of every team player and every statistic, and they scream, yell, cheer, and jump up and down for the players. In the same way, I have also known of people who spent the whole Sunday morning worship service dreaming about the local restaurant buffet they would visit as soon as church ended. The menu is memorized. Every item available has been tried, and there is even a regular table where they sit at every visit.

Is there something in your life that brings the excitement out in your heart? It could be a ballgame, a sale at the mall, a great buffet table, a daily soap opera, or anything at all. Each of us has a heart, and we know how to worship something. In fact, we are all worshiping something this very minute, but our hearts and our worship may be misplaced. Examine your heart today and begin to sing to the Lord. Give worship where it is deserved. Earthly pleasures will only last a moment, but His favor lasts a lifetime.

# God, where are You leading me today?

August 10

# Wallowing in the Pigpen

*"When he came to his senses, he said, 'How many of my father's hired men have food to spare, and here I am starving to death! I will set out and go back to my father and say to him: Father, I have sinned against heaven and against you. I am no longer worthy to be called your son; make me like one of your hired men.' So he got up and went to his father. But while he was still a long way off, his father saw him and was filled with compassion for him; he ran to his son, threw his arms around him and kissed him. The son said to him, 'Father, I have sinned against heaven and against you. I am no longer worthy to be called your son.' But the father said to his servants, 'Quick! Bring the best robe and put it on him. Put a ring on his finger and sandals on his feet.'"* —Luke 15:17–22

When the prodigal son got up, crawled out of the pigpen, and returned home to his father, he received the ring, the robe, and the prime rib dinner. You know, we often get angry at God for not presenting us with the ring, the robe, and the steak while we are still wallowing in the pigpen. We want Him to come to us, rather than humbly crawling to Him on our knees. Repent of that attitude, and praise God that He does not reward Sodom and Gomorrah. Even more, praise God that He *does* reward those who earnestly seek Him—check out the rings, robes, and banquet tables for the sons at home with God!

*August 11*

# God, where are You leading me today?

August 12

# Asking, Seeking, and Knocking

*"Ask and it will be given to you; seek and you will find; knock and the door will be opened to you. For everyone who asks receives; he who seeks finds; and to him who knocks, the door will be opened."* ⬤Matthew 7:7–8

I hope that you ask and seek and knock all the time on God's door to find out what His will is and to bring your requests before Him. God makes the best decisions, and He knows the best gifts and how to indulge you with them. If you will just be patient and obedient, the results will blow you away! Do not be afraid that if you wait on God, you will be disappointed. To the contrary, He will surprise you beyond your wildest dreams! All you need to do is ask and seek your Heavenly Father, and then obey His will for your life.

*August 13*

# God, where are You leading me today?

August 14

# Quit Making Excuses

by *Michael Shamblin*

*"The* LORD *does not look at the things man looks at. Man looks at the outward appearance, but the* LORD *looks at the heart."* ━1 Samuel 16:7b

These days, almost everyone seems to be trying to improve their physical appearance. While there is nothing wrong with trying to look better, there is something much more important that people need to work on. This is the heart. Now, I am not talking about the physical heart that pumps blood, but the *spiritual* heart. In many cases, the outside of the body is focused on while the most important part of the body is ignored! We need to work on getting our hearts right before God. We need to purify our hearts so God can dwell in us and work through us. Get rid of the sin in your life and quit making excuses to God, and then the other things will fall into place.

# God, where are You leading me today?

_August 16_

# Our Spiritual Act of Worship

*Therefore, I urge you, brothers, in view of God's mercy, to offer your bodies as living sacrifices, holy and pleasing to God—this is your spiritual act of worship. Do not conform any longer to the pattern of this world, but be transformed by the renewing of your mind. Then you will be able to test and approve what God's will is—his good, pleasing and perfect will.*

*—Romans 12:1–2*

Like everyone, I have suffered in my life. But instead of dwelling on my trials and hardships, I have grown into a happy, content person because of the suffering. I feel this way because I have learned never to defy or rebel against God's desert leadings—even when it means suffering. After all, it was God's will that Jesus should suffer on the cross, and because Jesus stepped forward and faced His suffering that day, I have received one of the greatest gifts from God that I could receive . . . forgiveness and a home in heaven with Him someday. Because of the personal suffering God has placed before me and because of the way He holds my hand as I stand to face the hardships, I know God so much better now. Even in the times when I don't have a clue about the specific reason for my suffering, I trust completely that God knows what He is up to.

*August 17*

# God, where are You leading me today?

August 18

# Love for God Grows

*"Because of the increase of wickedness, the love of most will grow cold, but he who stands firm to the end will be saved."* ➤Matthew 24:12–13

If you think a crush on God may go away and be replaced by a "more mature," emotionless love, think again. Your love for food grows more and more. Statistics show us that people in developed countries are getting larger and larger and more and more passionate for their food. According to most conservative estimates, at the rate we are going, half the population will be overweight in the next 20 years. Have you noticed that the older you get, the harder it is to lose weight? That's because you become increasingly attached to what you adore. So love *does* grow—even the love for food.

As for me, my love for *God* has grown more and more. I can't get Him out of my heart and mind. It is a passion, and that is how God wants it. Matthew 6:24 states, "No one can serve two masters." Why? Because you only have one heart, and it was made to be devoted to one master. Had the children of God stayed in Egypt, they would have become more and more enslaved. If you keep obeying the food, five years from now you will be even more attached to the food than you are right now. But if you start devoting your heart to God today, then five years from now you will be even more attached to Him. The next time you see me, I will be even more deeply in love with God—how exciting!

*August 19*

# God, where are You leading me today?

*August 20*

# Do Not Save Yourself

*The people stood watching, and the rulers even sneered at him. They said, "He saved others; let him save himself if he is the Christ of God, the Chosen One." The soldiers also came up and mocked him. They offered him wine vinegar and said, "If you are the king of the Jews, save yourself." There was a written notice above him, which read: THIS IS THE KING OF THE JEWS. One of the criminals who hung there hurled insults at him: "Aren't you the Christ? Save yourself and us!"* ━Luke 23:35–39

Throughout the ministry of Jesus, He was mocked, scorned, and tested. He could have saved Himself from any of these trials at any time, but He did not. Then, on the day when Jesus hung on the cross, He was tempted by others three times to save Himself from the pain and suffering He was enduring. Again, He refused. He knew it was more important to look to God. If God wanted to save Him, He would. But it was God's will that Jesus suffer so that many could be saved.

As you are feeling the hot desert testing right now, I'm sure you will be tempted to save yourself from your suffering. You may want to give yourself more food than God has decided to give you. But stop and think a minute before you do. Look to Jesus Christ for the perfect example of being strong under temptation. Pray to our Almighty Father and let Him decide. Then you will have eternal salvation. Jesus sits at the right-hand side of God. They are dear companions.

*August 21*

# God, where are You leading me today?

August 22

# Is He Your Lord?

*"You shall not misuse the name of the LORD your God, for the LORD will not hold anyone guiltless who misuses his name."* ━Exodus 20:7

You should never call the Lord "Lord" when He is *not* the Lord of your life. Before you say, "But He *is* my Lord," consider this for a minute. If you do not consult Him about everything, or if you refuse to obey His commands, or if you cannot give Him your whole heart, then He is not your Lord. You can't just call Him a name like "Lord" if you do not follow through with your heart, your mind, and your actions. If you call Him "Lord" while you are bowing down to other idols on this earth, you will confuse many people and be a stumbling block to those who are trying to figure out the relationship they should have with God. We should take His role in our lives very seriously, and we should never misuse His honorable and glorious name.

*August 23*

# God, where are You leading me today?

*August 24*

# Come . . . Let Us Worship Him!

*"We saw his star in the east and have come to worship him."*
—*Matthew 2:2b*

Who, or what, have you come to worship? Do you behold or adore the praise of other people? Then you have missed the mark. Do you behold or adore food? Then you will become like a refrigerator. Do you behold or adore money and material possessions? Then you will be greedy and alone. But . . . do you behold and adore Christ? Then you will be fulfilled. You will become like Christ at heart, serving and worshiping the Father. As the men in the verse above saw His star in the east and traveled a distance to worship Him, we also should look for His signs, always seek to be near Him, and worship Him above all things. Psalm 34:5 tells us, "those who look to him are radiant; their faces are never covered with shame." So come . . . let us worship Him!

# God, where are You leading me today?

# God Will Satisfy You

*"But you would be fed with the finest of wheat; with honey from the rock I would satisfy you."* —Psalm 81:16

We should never question God's ability to satisfy us. After all, in Matthew 7:9–11, Jesus says, "Which of you, if his son asks for bread, will give him a stone? Or if he asks for a fish, will give him a snake? If you, then, though you are evil, know how to give good gifts to your children, how much more will your Father in heaven give good gifts to those who ask him!" Those of us who are parents know the wonderful feeling we get when we provide for our children and see them trust in us to take care of them. God wants to provide for us in the same way. And not just our food, shelter, and clothing, but the things we *truly* need—love, acceptance, and security. God knows how to satisfy His children. Trust in His promises and let Him satisfy your hungry heart.

*August 27*

# God, where are You leading me today?

*August 28*

# David's Undignified Dance

*David, wearing a linen ephod, danced before the LORD with all his might, while he and the entire house of Israel brought up the ark of the LORD with shouts and the sound of trumpets. When David returned home to bless his household, Michal daughter of Saul came out to meet him and said, "How the king of Israel has distinguished himself today, disrobing in the sight of the slave girls of his servants as any vulgar fellow would!" David said to Michal, "It was before the LORD, who chose me rather than your father or anyone from his house when he appointed me ruler over the LORD's people Israel—I will celebrate before the LORD. I will become even more undignified than this, and I will be humiliated in my own eyes. But by these slave girls you spoke of, I will be held in honor."* ➤2 Samuel 6:14–15,20–22

David so loved the Father that he would dance in the streets even though he was a king. We learn later in this story that because Saul's daughter questioned and ridiculed King David's actions, she was stricken by God so that she could never have children. David's explanation to her about why he was dancing in the street was simple— he was celebrating before the Lord. You see, when you open your heart fully to God, the feeling can be overwhelming. You won't care what other people think about your thoughts or actions or the words that you speak as you praise the Lord. You may be seen as imperfect or even foolish in the eyes of people whose hearts are not devoted to the Father, but God will see your passion, and you will be praised and rewarded for it. One other point we can learn from this story: Don't make fun of how others show their passionate love for God—just imitate it!

*August 29*

# God, where are You leading me today?

_August 30_

# Serving the Whims

*It is not fitting for a fool to live in luxury—how much worse for a slave to rule over princes!* ━Proverbs 19:10

We claim that we love God's law . . . but do we? Many of you right now live in a home that is completely upside down, where the children rule the parents. The parents are invited by the children to get with the program or get out of their way. They completely manipulate and use the parents. How does even a one-year-old know that he can accomplish this? Because the child can sense that the parent desires fellowship at almost any cost. The parent adores the child, and the child adores himself—a nice combination for getting what you want. The parent jumps at the child's yelling or pouting, not vice versa.

How difficult it is to discipline someone whom you adore. Many of you have struggled with a spoiled child, I am sure. If the child would only *submit*, there would be peace and blessings for that child. Oh, but no . . . temper tantrums, sarcasm, manipulation, anger, demands, and a tossing of the head are all you receive from the spoiled child. This is a very sick situation to have the creator or parent—the one who brought the child into life—bowing down to the fancy of the child. If it were not for the parent, there would be no child! Yet, the parent serves not only the needs, but the whims of the child.

How awkward to see a parent jumping for a child, or the owner of a business bowing down to the employees, or a husband bowing down to his wife, or a king waiting on his servants as they sit on his throne and demand more from him. All of these pictures make me want to shout out: "Improper! Immoral! Inappropriate! Unseemly!" You must show God that you *do* love His law by getting His laws back in order.

*August 31*

# God, where are You leading me today?

September 1

# Causing a Delay

*Aaron answered them, "Take off the gold earrings that your wives, your sons and your daughters are wearing, and bring them to me." So all the people took off their earrings and brought them to Aaron. He took what they handed him and made it into an idol cast in the shape of a calf, fashioning it with a tool. Then they said, "These are your gods, O Israel, who brought you up out of Egypt."*　　　　　　　　　　　　　　　　　*━Exodus 32:2–4*

*When I looked, I saw that you had sinned against the* LORD *your God; you had made for yourselves an idol cast in the shape of a calf. You had turned aside quickly from the way that the* LORD *had commanded you. So I took the two tablets and threw them out of my hands, breaking them to pieces before your eyes.*　　　　　　　　　　　　　　　*━Deuteronomy 9:16–17*

When considerable time had passed and the Israelites did not see Moses coming back, so as not to bother God and in case His watch was broken, they made a golden calf to help speed things up. Of course, Israel's worship of the golden calf made God angry. Moses—angry himself—threw down the tablets God had made, breaking them. The Israelites had to wait another 40 days for Moses as he replaced the tablets.

We are no different from the Israelites. We, too, are willing to give up our jewelry to keep paying for our false gods and false helpers. We carve out an exercise and diet pill regimen to speed up our journey because we do not want to eat less food—we love the food too much to eat less of it. We say, "I won't tell Gwen, but I'm going to mix Weigh Down with diet pills to get out of this desert faster." But I warn you, you will only delay your progress and stay in the desert longer.

We should learn from the Israelites and their false god. Truth bears out that our false gods sabotage us rather than save us! Trying to worship God and food at the same time

*September 2*

will never work. God is jealous and knows that these false helpers will not help you stop loving your stronghold. You will never truly succeed and be content until you turn to God as the Great Physician. Instead of quickly turning *away* from Him, turn quickly *toward* the Father.

God, where are You leading me today?

_____

_____

_____

_____

_____

_____

_____

_____

_____

_____

_____

_____

_____

_____

_____

_____

_____

_____

_____

*September 3*

# Pursue His Righteousness and His Love

*He who pursues righteousness and love finds life, prosperity and honor.*
*⟶Proverbs 21:21*

D o you ever feel as if nothing is going right, no matter how hard you are working or trying? You work so hard to find personal success, financial wealth, and popularity among your peers, but no matter how much success, wealth, or popularity you achieve, you will never feel truly satisfied . . . it won't be enough. But if you give your life over to God first, things will turn out much differently. If you pursue His righteousness and if you pursue His love, there is nothing that He won't give from His storehouse up above. So no matter what you are seeking, God can give you wonderful gifts if you just pursue His will for your life above all else, and let Him handle all the details!

*Giver of Things*
*by Gwen Shamblin*

*You are the One that I adore*
*I praise You day by day*
*You are my love, my heart I pour*
*Because You light my way*

*Since You are my love, I hear Your call*
*You waken me in the night*
*When I respond I read Your law*
*And darkness turns to light*

*If I pursue Your righteousness*
*And if I pursue Your love*
*There's nothing that You wouldn't give*
*From storehouses up above*

CHORUS: *How could I feel this way*
*Because You're the King of kings*
*How could I feel this great*
*Because You are the Giver of things*

*September 4*

# God, where are You leading me today?

September 5

# You Are Chosen

*We have not received the spirit of the world but the Spirit who is from God, that we may understand what God has freely given us. This is what we speak, not in words taught us by human wisdom but in words taught by the Spirit, expressing spiritual truths in spiritual words. The man without the Spirit does not accept the things that come from the Spirit of God, for they are foolishness to him, and he cannot understand them, because they are spiritually discerned. The spiritual man makes judgments about all things, but he himself is not subject to any man's judgment: "For who has known the mind of the Lord that he may instruct him?" But we have the mind of Christ.* ━1 Corinthians 2:12–16

When you understand that God's grace is giving you the opportunity through Jesus Christ to fall in love with Him, then you have "spiritual discernment." For some people, this is foolishness; it is too simple; it doesn't sound complicated enough for an impressive sermon. Satan would love to keep the simple, wholehearted love for God as "foolishness" so that the sheep will not find this precious green grass. This green grass is sweet and simple and brings life eternal. Please be wary of teachers who make God out to want more than your pure heart of love.

*September 6*

# God, where are You leading me today?

*September 7*

# Consider Each Command

*Love must be sincere. Hate what is evil; cling to what is good. Be devoted to one another in brotherly love. Honor one another above yourselves. Never be lacking in zeal, but keep your spiritual fervor, serving the Lord. Be joyful in hope, patient in affliction, faithful in prayer. Share with God's people who are in need. Practice hospitality.* ━Romans 12:9–13

The Bible is absolutely packed with awesome information and direction. There is so much true nutrition for the heart and soul that some paragraphs in the Bible take a whole week to absorb. This one is like that. Spend some time with these words. Consider each command. What are we being asked to do? What does it mean to be devoted, to honor, to keep our spiritual fervor? Why is God telling us to share with His people and practice hospitality? God would never ask us to do anything or to direct our hearts in a certain direction unless it was truly important to Him. Today, take a few minutes and evaluate your own life in regard to the above scripture.

*September 8*

# God, where are You leading me today?

*September 9*

# He Wants to Save Us

*"You were wearied by all your ways, but you would not say, 'It is hopeless.'*
*You found renewal of your strength, and so you did not faint. I will expose*
*your righteousness and your works, and they will not benefit you."*
—Isaiah 57:10,12

People who keep using their own strength to get by are not new. These people just keep trying plan after plan, certain that the next one will work. They refuse to admit that the situation is hopeless unless they have help from above. What they fail to realize is that nothing will work without God's will. God wants us to turn to Him for our plans and our actions. *He* wants to be the one to give us strength and success; He wants to be our Savior! This is why none of our man-made schemes or plans will ever work permanently unless we go to God first and ask for His guidance and His help. If you are trying to lose weight or let go of a stronghold *for* Him but not *with* Him, you are still using your own strength so that you can feed your *ego.* Let go of your ego and pride and depend upon the strength of God like an infant in a mother's arms.

# God, where are You leading me today?

September 11

# The Gentleman of All Gentlemen

*To him who struck down the firstborn of Egypt {His love endures forever.}*
*and brought Israel out from among them      {His love endures forever.}*
*with a mighty hand and outstretched arm;      {His love endures forever.}*
*to him who divided the Red Sea asunder      {His love endures forever.}*
*and brought Israel through the midst of it,      {His love endures forever.}*
*but swept Pharaoh and his army into the Red Sea;*
*                                                                  {His love endures forever.}*
*to him who led his people through the desert,   {His love endures forever.}*
*and who gives food to every creature.        {His love endures forever.}*
*Psalm 136:10–16,25*

God led His children down to Egypt, and then He shook the earth and rescued the Israelites from the clutches of Pharaoh. God then parted the Red Sea and took His children across on dry land into the desert with Himself. God never left their presence, for He remained close in the form of a cloud by day and fire by night. He set up examinations for their heart, put up with the grumbling, prepared disciplining measures for them, and fed them daily with manna from heaven above. God was faithful in battle after battle. And yet, He saw that His love and His faithfulness were not enough to pull the heartstrings of mankind to total devotion and love in return. God moved even closer as the Word became flesh and dwelt among man. And even though we showed Him how we really felt by annihilating Him, He remained faithful and desirous of our love. God is the gentleman of all gentlemen, and even in the midst of the grief we give Him, He remains faithful. Praise Him!

*September 12*

# God, where are You leading me today?

September 13

# The One Mighty God

*The Mighty One, God, the LORD, speaks and summons the earth from the rising of the sun to the place where it sets.* —*Psalm 50:1*

God controls everything. He has all the power. He is the Creator of the entire earth. So why do you think you will lose time and money if you spend your efforts laying down the worship of a false idol? You will not lose time. Each minute you spend turning your love for a stronghold into love for God will be given back to you, and more. God does not want your money, because He is a multibillionaire, and so He will reward you with everything you need. You see, God can give all these things back to you, because He is a God—a true God—and He does not *need* your time or money. So when you give of yourself to Him, He will generously give back. No false idol on this earth can do that. Only the one and only, true, honest-to-goodness GOD!

*September 14*

# God, where are You leading me today?

_September 15_

# The Great Surgeon

*"And you, my son Solomon, acknowledge the God of your father, and serve him with wholehearted devotion and with a willing mind, for the LORD searches every heart and understands every motive behind the thoughts. If you seek him, he will be found by you; but if you forsake him, he will reject you forever."* —1 Chronicles 28:9

As you go through the journey in the desert, you may realize several things about your heart that have not occurred to you before. God knows all your thoughts and motives, and He will show you exactly what you have been giving your heart to. His hot desert acts as an X-ray machine, revealing the inner workings of the heart. Don't be afraid for your heart to be revealed. When the Great Surgeon is performing major surgery on your heart, He is making a large incision, removing the pain and the sickness. When He is finished, you have a strong new heart, able to beat with love for Him!

_____

_____

_____

_____

_____

_____

_____

_____

_____

_____

_____

_____

*September 16*

# God, where are You leading me today?

*September 17*

# Are You Bearing Good Fruit?

*By their fruit you will recognize them. Do people pick grapes from thorn-bushes, or figs from thistles? Likewise every good tree bears good fruit, but a bad tree bears bad fruit. A good tree cannot bear bad fruit, and a bad tree cannot bear good fruit. Thus, by their fruit you will recognize them.*
*—Matthew 7:16–18,20*

You will be sorely attacked when your heart is truly abiding in the Vine. You will be falsely accused, and there will be enemies. You will be able to write your own set of Psalms before it is time for you to return home to the Father. When the world falsely accuses you and tries to make you out as the troublemaker when you are surely bringing the sheep back to the Father, the only thing you can hang on to is the *fruit*. Now, these worldly people I am referring to usually attend church every week and can quote scripture just as Satan did to Jesus during His time in the desert. You must look to the Father and check the fruit of your own life: love, joy, peace, patience, kindness, goodness, and self-control. Next, look at the fruit of repentance born in others' lives as a result of your loving them on the Father's behalf. Please do not get discouraged in doing good and keep your eyes on the great crowd of witnesses that underwent so much persecution for the sake of Jesus Christ.

P.S. Check out the fruit of those who accuse the righteous, and you will find that they have no peace, patience, kindness, etc., but rather are filled with malice, jealousy, anger, rage, greed, and haughtiness.

# God, where are You leading me today?

September 19

# The Right Kind of Fear

*When the people saw the thunder and lightning and heard the trumpet and saw the mountain in smoke, they trembled with fear. They stayed at a distance and said to Moses, "Speak to us yourself and we will listen. But do not have God speak to us or we will die." Moses said to the people, "Do not be afraid. God has come to test you, so that the fear of God will be with you to keep you from sinning."* —Exodus 20:18–20

Now, that was a strange statement: "Do not be *afraid*. God has come to test you, so that the *fear* of God will be with you to keep you from sinning." It was God, trying once more to create an inside force in the heart of man, to place the fear of God in your heart so that you will not want to sin. However, you should not be afraid. In other words, don't have an outside force of fear that just terrifies you. That kind of fear doesn't invoke love. But the right kind of fear, an inside force in your heart, can keep you from sinning!

# God, where are You leading me today?

September 21

# "See to It"

*"No one lights a lamp and puts it in a place where it will be hidden, or under a bowl. Instead he puts it on its stand, so that those who come in may see the light. Your eye is the lamp of your body. When your eyes are good, your whole body also is full of light. But when they are bad, your body also is full of darkness. See to it, then, that the light within you is not darkness. Therefore, if your whole body is full of light, and no part of it dark, it will be completely lighted, as when the light of a lamp shines on you."*
*—Luke 11:33–36*

Someone who loves God more than anything is a lamp and should be put on a stand to give light to everyone in God's house. Each of us has this opportunity to shine as a lamp for God. This opportunity is already within us. But then Jesus warns us to *see to it* that the light within us is not darkness. So it is not just an opportunity to shine for the Lord, but it is a direction from Jesus. He is warning us that we should never become overly confident that our hearts are pure and our lights shine bright. Instead, we should stay on our knees and in His word to be diligent that there is no darkness in our hearts.

*September 22*

# God, where are You leading me today?

_September 23_

# The Opportunity in the Desert

*How often they rebelled against him in the desert and grieved him in the wasteland! Again and again they put God to the test; they vexed the Holy One of Israel. They did not remember his power—the day he redeemed them from the oppressor, the day he displayed his miraculous signs in Egypt....*
*—Psalm 78:40–43a*

When you leave Egypt, you really experience how much of your heart is buried in the pyramids, which are presently in the shape of a pantry and a refrigerator. God has brought you to the desert—a place designed for just you and Him, with no room for worldly idols. But you learn something about your heart in the desert, far away from the familiar food scene. Your heart is not satisfied with just God. God alone isn't enough, and you want more. You want your food, too. It is a tough lesson to learn, but if you remain focused on God, you will succeed. This desert of testing is an opportunity—not a curse—an *opportunity* to learn much about the Father and yourself. As you learn these things about yourself and you give your heart, soul, mind, and strength to the Father, He will give you everything back. His rewards will be great, and you will sing of His glory!

_____

_____

_____

_____

_____

_____

_____

*September 24*

# God, where are You leading me today?

September 25

# Put Your Children in His Hands

*In bitterness of soul Hannah wept much and prayed to the LORD. And she made a vow, saying, "O LORD Almighty, if you will only look upon your servant's misery and remember me, and not forget your servant but give her a son, then I will give him to the LORD for all the days of his life, and no razor will ever be used on his head."* —1 Samuel 1:10–11

*He answered, "While the child was still alive, I fasted and wept. I thought, 'Who knows? The LORD may be gracious to me and let the child live.' But now that he is dead, why should I fast? Can I bring him back again? I will go to him, but he will not return to me."* —2 Samuel 12:22–23

If you are a parent, God has placed you in a position of authority and caregiving over your children. But you must remember that they are, first and foremost, *His* children, and He will provide for them in all ways. Like Hannah, you must be willing to say to God that your children belong to Him for all the days of their lives. Be in constant prayer for guidance about how to raise, discipline, and teach your children, for God alone has the perfect plan.

You must also be at peace about God's will for your children. Like David, pray for the strength, health, and safety of your children, but if God's plan is different, accept His will with faith and trust, and He will comfort your soul. If you follow God's plan for you as a parent by seeking His guidance in loving, teaching, and disciplining your children, you will be on the right path. Even during times when you feel as if the world is passing you and your children by, if you have chosen this path, you will look up and see that your children's gifts are many, their relationship with God is strong, and their days are filled with peace and joy!

*September 26*

# God, where are You leading me today?

September 27

# Like Mother, Like Daughter
# Like Father, Like Son

*I have been reminded of your sincere faith, which first lived in your grand-mother Lois and in your mother Eunice and, I am persuaded, now lives in you also.* ➝ 2 Timothy 1:5
*"Everyone who quotes proverbs will quote this proverb about you: 'Like mother, like daughter.'"* ➝ Ezekiel 16:44

Besides the misplaced devotion to food, parents often secretly hold within their hearts the pursuit of money and the praise of men. Children will pick up on the diametric goals of the parents who go to church and yet pursue money or social climbing. If only parents could see that they are forcing the ungodly and unrewarding occupation of money and praise on their children. God will only frustrate their goals. These confused parents want to live vicariously through their children, because they are greedy for attention and praise from mankind. When parents mistakenly create goals for their children that are not "forsaking-all-and-knowing-Christ" goals, then by the time the children are teens, they are very confused, unhappy, and emotional, often having fits of anger and tears. Depression surfaces from time to time when they stop to realize that they are empty and getting nowhere. These children soon mimic their parents' pursuits, spending their energy and strength to strive toward worldly goals every day. They expect that they can "make" things happen for them with their own raw talent. Pride sets in. A little god is birthed and, as the old saying goes, "like mother, like daughter—like father, like son." We must check our own hearts and motives!

*September 28*

# God, where are You leading me today?

*September 29*

# Finding the Right Path

*I am your servant; give me discernment that I may understand your statutes. It is time for you to act, O LORD; your law is being broken. Because I love your commands more than gold, more than pure gold, and because I consider all your precepts right, I hate every wrong path.*
*——Psalm 119:125–128*

The Bible helps us find the right path that will lead us straight to the heart of the Father. It helps us circumvent the mountains and valleys, and it provides street lamps for dark paths. It will help us avoid the dreadful parts of the desert that are thirsty and waterless. It will help us evade the scorpions, snakes, sandpits, and desert storms. If we do not stay in His Word and honor His precepts—shouting them from the street corners, writing them on the doorposts, and talking about them when we are going in and coming out—then, my friends, we will forfeit peace, and it will cost us dearly at times. If we are not careful, we might rewalk some of the wicked desert paths that the Israelites walked. Therefore, we must learn from history.

*September 30*

# God, where are You leading me today?

October 1

# Don't Look Back

*"Woe to the obstinate children," declares the* LORD, *"to those who carry out plans that are not mine, forming an alliance, but not by my Spirit, heaping sin upon sin; who go down to Egypt without consulting me; who look for help to Pharaoh's protection, to Egypt's shade for refuge. But Pharaoh's protection will be to your shame, Egypt's shade will bring you disgrace."*
—Isaiah 30:1–3

God has delivered you from having to serve your strongholds and false idols, and now you have the chance to serve Him. Times may get tough . . . it's all part of the hot desert. But don't even think about going back to Egypt, depending upon the aid of man or pills or other things to "save you" from your situation. Where does your mind go when the scales go up or you backslide on your stronghold? *That* is your Egypt.

If you are tempted, take time to remember all the trials and bondage of being enslaved to your stronghold, such as constant diets, denied foods, mandatory exercise routines, and clothes that don't fit. There is nothing there for you in Egypt, and you will regret the wasted time you spend relying upon a nothing, a false help. Spare yourself the trouble—trust in God, and don't look back to Egypt! God and Jesus are your Savior!

# God, where are You leading me today?

October 3

# Everything We Need for Life

*His divine power has given us everything we need for life and godliness through our knowledge of him who called us by his own glory and goodness. Through these he has given us his very great and precious promises, so that through them you may participate in the divine nature and escape the corruption in the world caused by evil desires.* ⚊2 Peter 1:3–4

Quit looking for one more person or book or formula that is going to make you lose the weight or that will help you with your stronghold. Don't you see? Through God, we have everything we need for life and godliness. Everything! He has given us a means by which we can escape the corruption caused by our evil desires. So why do we continue to seek other methods? Methods such as constant dieting do not help us escape our evil desires, but only lead us farther into them by making us fall more in love with the food! God has already given you what you need for godliness. So stop digging for oil in the wrong place. You will strike oil when you look up and get your answers from above.

# God, where are You leading me today?

# The Four Soils
## (The Four Hearts)

*Then he told them many things in parables, saying: "A farmer went out to sow his seed. As he was scattering the seed, some fell along the path, and the birds came and ate it up. Some fell on rocky places, where it did not have much soil. It sprang up quickly, because the soil was shallow. But when the sun came up, the plants were scorched, and they withered because they had no root. Other seed fell among thorns, which grew up and choked the plants. Still other seed fell on good soil, where it produced a crop—a hundred, sixty or thirty times what was sown. He who has ears, let him hear."*
*—Matthew 13:3–9*

I think I have figured out one of the reasons that some people feel at arm's length with God. Read what Jesus said about the four soils. This can actually describe the different types of hearts on this earth. You see, the seed is God's kingdom of love, the soil is a heart of love, and the rock is a heart of hate, the antithesis of love. Love cannot root in hate. In the first heart, the seeds were scattered—not even listened to or given a chance. The second heart had some ability to respond to the love, and the love sprouted toward God, but because hate, malice, jealousy, and anger were solidly fixed in the rocky heart, the love could not take root. The third soil was a heart of love . . . but it also loved the world . . . but it loved God . . . but it loved the world . . . but it loved God. At first, it grew in love toward the Father and became a plant; but where the heart is divided, the world will always win, and the world squeezed out the love for the Father. We must believe in God. Repent from these behaviors that are the antithesis of a belief in God and watch your heart grow in love. Watch His kingdom grow in your heart, like the good heart that produced fruit a hundredfold!

*October 6*

# God, where are You leading me today?

# Look for the Oasis

*"'You yourselves have seen what I did to Egypt, and how I carried you on eagles' wings and brought you to myself.'"* —Exodus 19:4

God rescued the Israelites from Egypt and then started testing them right off the bat. For the first three days of wandering in the desert, they found no water. When they finally did find water, it was too bitter to drink. They failed the trust test, but God still miraculously made the water sweet and then led them to not one, but *twelve,* springs of water and seventy palm trees.

This desert exam—even though it was resolved and followed by an oasis—never sank into the hearts of the Israelites. They never connected that God was going to take them to the edge of death and then rescue them at the twelfth hour. Are you learning that God will take you to the edge of death with your stronghold and then rescue you in an amazing way? You will experience desert oasis after desert oasis, over and over. Learn to trust Him.

*October 8*

# God, where are You leading me today?

October 9

# Weak-willed Hearts

*"'How weak-willed you are, declares the Sovereign Lord, when you do all these things, acting like a brazen prostitute!'"* —Ezekiel 16:30
*They . . . gain control over weak-willed women, who are loaded down with sins and are swayed by all kinds of evil desires.* —2 Timothy 3:6

Weak-willed is neither male nor female, even though some passages in the Bible refer specifically to women. Weak-willed hearts become magnetized to the latest thing or person that they see. They have no individual definition or direction and are easily swayed. They have no goal of their own. The weak-willed person goes along with the crowd because they have not thought through the situation for themselves.

To develop a stronger will in your heart, you have to focus on Jesus Christ and call upon Him constantly so that you can maintain your focus. You need more time alone with God. You should not depend on Sunday morning service alone to keep you strong all week long. You also have to be aware of the company you keep, because bad company corrupts good morals. You must imagine yourself turning others down when they are trying to lead you astray. Once you develop a stronger will with God's help, you have a better chance of avoiding being swayed by all kinds of evil desires.

*October 10*

# God, where are You leading me today?

October 11

# A Treasured Possession

*"'Now if you obey me fully and keep my covenant, then out of all nations you will be my treasured possession. Although the whole earth is mine, you will be for me a kingdom of priests and a holy nation.'"* ═Exodus 19:5–6a

As time goes by, some of us might find ourselves plateaued in the desert. The next thing we know, we haven't lost weight for weeks, which may turn into months, which may turn into years. We have thought that since we have plateaued and are feeling pain again after the honeymoon, it must be the heat of the desert. We say: "Oh, it's just one of those desert storms. God is just working on me. I'm waiting on the Lord. He is working on something else in my life right now. He will complete the work He started."

Yes, you will struggle in the desert, but true desert struggles are the pain and suffering from *obedience*, not the pain that comes from hugging the refrigerator and trying to get God to repent or change His mind so that you can have two masters. Desert pain is not the pain of disobedience! Remember, those who were disobedient died in the desert. But if you obey His commands, you will be a treasured possession.

# God, where are You leading me today?

October 13

# Vine and Branches

*"I am the vine; you are the branches. If a man remains in me and I in him, he will bear much fruit; apart from me you can do nothing. If anyone does not remain in me, he is like a branch that is thrown away and withers; such branches are picked up, thrown into the fire and burned. If you remain in me and my words remain in you, ask whatever you wish, and it will be given you."* ─John 15:5–7

It is one thing to *find* a man, but it is another thing to *keep* a man. It is one thing to *come* to Christ, but it is another thing to *remain* in Christ. Both the King James Version and the New King James Version of the Bible use the phrase "abide in me." Christ said "if" you abide in Him. If you do not remain in Him (and obviously you have the choice not to), then the picture is not pretty. You need to stay totally focused on the mind and heart of Jesus Christ. "Abide" or "remain" means to stick around—to stay put. The branches get all of their life from the vine. They get all the material they need for life from one source. Likewise, we cannot look for life in multiple places. You know when you have figured out what "abide" means, because your prayers will be answered constantly.

*October 14*

# God, where are You leading me today?

October 15

# Has Your Conscience Been Seared?

*Such teachings come through hypocritical liars, whose consciences have been seared as with a hot iron.* ━1 Timothy 4:2

*So I tell you this, and insist on it in the Lord, that you must no longer live as the Gentiles do, in the futility of their thinking. They are darkened in their understanding and separated from the life of God because of the ignorance that is in them due to the hardening of their hearts. Having lost all sensitivity, they have given themselves over to sensuality so as to indulge in every kind of impurity, with a continual lust for more. You, however, did not come to know Christ that way. Surely you heard of him and were taught in him in accordance with the truth that is in Jesus. You were taught, with regard to your former way of life, to put off your old self, which is being corrupted by its deceitful desires; to be made new in the attitude of your minds; and to put on the new self, created to be like God in true righteousness and holiness. Therefore each of you must put off falsehood and speak truthfully to his neighbor, for we are all members of one body. "In your anger do not sin": Do not let the sun go down while you are still angry, and do not give the devil a foothold.* ━Ephesians 4:17–27

Many will beg God to please love them but let them keep their other loves too! If we continue in sinful behavior, we will eventually become calloused and have no more guilty feelings because our conscience will have been seared. What a frightening thought! Take it from me, you do not want it both ways—you will be miserable.

Jesus redeemed us and set us apart to love the Father. In Titus 2 we learn that Jesus gave Himself to redeem us from all wickedness and to purify God's people, and that because of this, we should be eager to do what is pleasing to God. So each of us must put on our new self—this self that has been given to us through God's grace. We were made to do this.

*October 16*

# God, where are You leading me today?

_October 17_

# Desert Discipline

*And you have forgotten that word of encouragement that addresses you as sons: "My son, do not make light of the Lord's discipline, and do not lose heart when he rebukes you, because the Lord disciplines those he loves, and he punishes everyone he accepts as a son." Endure hardship as discipline; God is treating you as sons. For what son is not disciplined by his father? If you are not disciplined (and everyone undergoes discipline), then you are illegitimate children and not true sons. Moreover, we have all had human fathers who disciplined us and we respected them for it. How much more should we submit to the Father of our spirits and live! Our fathers disciplined us for a little while as they thought best; but God disciplines us for our good, that we may share in his holiness. No discipline seems pleasant at the time, but painful. Later on, however, it produces a harvest of righteousness and peace for those who have been trained by it.* ⟶Hebrews 12:5–11*

The desert is a place of discipline. That doesn't mean that you are a failure. Satan loves for you to think that you are, and he loves for you to ignore the fact that you are a prize to be won. But God disciplines His children out of love and concern. However, Satan knows that you can get distracted easily and mistake the discipline of God for a lack of love. How "opposite world" can you get! Stick to the truth, and don't listen to anything the king of lies has to say. Anyone investing attention toward you loves you, and who has invested more attention in you during your lifetime than the great God Almighty?

*October 18*

# God, where are You leading me today?

October 19

# Wholehearted Devotion

*Be diligent in these matters; give yourself wholly to them, so that everyone may see your progress. Watch your life and doctrine closely. Persevere in them, because if you do, you will save both yourself and your hearers.*
*—1 Timothy 4:15–16*
*I am saying this for your own good, not to restrict you, but that you may live in a right way in undivided devotion to the Lord.*
*—1 Corinthians 7:35*

If you believe in something, you will want to surround yourself totally with its teaching—absorbing, imitating, and baptizing yourself into the philosophy. For many of us, what we have believed in for so long are the man-made diet rules and regulations. We have studied every new diet, analyzed every bite of food, and committed to memory various exercise routines. But now you have something new to believe in. Instead of throwing yourself into any more diet books, food measurements, and fat grams, throw yourself into absorbing the life, the heart, and the love of Jesus. The rewards will be more fulfilling than you can imagine! No matter what your obsession, start today by transferring the same behavior over to God and His Word.

*October 20*

# God, where are You leading me today?

October 21

# Leave Room for God's Wrath

*Do not repay anyone evil for evil. Be careful to do what is right in the eyes of everybody. If it is possible, as far as it depends on you, live at peace with everyone. Do not take revenge, my friends, but leave room for God's wrath, for it is written: "It is mine to avenge; I will repay," says the Lord. On the contrary: "If your enemy is hungry, feed him; if he is thirsty, give him something to drink. In doing this, you will heap burning coals on his head." Do not be overcome by evil, but overcome evil with good.*

—Romans 12:17–21

Give up your need to win verbally. Stay peaceful and confident that God will take care of others who are doing wrong to you. God will be quick to correct and take revenge if you give Him room, but He does not gang up on people—if you talk back or take revenge, then He won't get involved. Another hint is this: He will not let your clever words or defense be effective. *He* wants to take care of us *Himself*, so put away your pocketknife and let Him use His powerful sword and His enormous army!

*October 22*

# God, where are You leading me today?

October 23

# Make Music in Your Heart

*Sing for joy to God our strength; shout aloud to the God of Jacob! Begin the music, strike the tambourine, play the melodious harp and lyre.*
                                                    ⟿*Psalm 81:1–2*

*Speak to one another with psalms, hymns and spiritual songs. Sing and make music in your heart to the Lord.*          ⟿*Ephesians 5:19*

King Saul would summon David to come and play the harp and sing to drive the evil spirits away. Satan is very jealous, and he cannot stand to hear the saints sing to the Father. There are many references urging us to sing to God and shout to God and to begin the music and strike the tambourine. I have never needed prompting for this command, because God has the perfect blend of leadership, genius, and power, as well as kindness and thoughtfulness. How can I help but sing praises to Him in joy? We all need to do more of it, even if we don't think we can sing, and even while we are in the hot desert!

*October 24*

# God, where are You leading me today?

October 25

# "Is the Lord Among Us or Not?"

*The LORD answered Moses, "Walk on ahead of the people. Take with you some of the elders of Israel and take in your hand the staff with which you struck the Nile, and go. I will stand there before you by the rock at Horeb. Strike the rock, and water will come out of it for the people to drink." So Moses did this in the sight of the elders of Israel. And he called the place Massah and Meribah because the Israelites quarreled and because they tested the LORD saying, "Is the LORD among us or not?"* ━Exodus 17:5–7

Let's dissect this new attitude. Their big question is— "Is the Lord among us or not?" Now, I don't think for one minute that the children of God didn't believe that God existed. That was not the problem. Look at the Israelites' question again: "Is the Lord among us or not?" What could they possibly be talking about? Could it be that these arrogant children of God were saying, "Is God *with* us or not?"—or better yet—"Is He going to get with the program or not? He is either with us or against us. Is God going to submit to our wants or not?" They had no use for a God who was not going to serve their cravings. So they were not so sure that Jehovah was working out! Is God among us or not?!

The state of the heart of man is more unmanageable and unruly than first thought; there are hearts that actually want God to *repent* if He is going to hang around! After all, they always have Egypt to run to if God doesn't give them what they want! We should make sure that we don't ever ask God to repent or make Him angry by asking Him to do things our way.

# God, where are You leading me today?

*October 27*

# Exchanging Our God

*"Therefore I bring charges against you again," declares the LORD. "And I will bring charges against your children's children. Cross over to the coasts of Kittim and look, send to Kedar and observe closely; see if there has ever been anything like this: Has a nation ever changed its gods? (Yet they are not gods at all.) But my people have exchanged their Glory for worthless idols. Be appalled at this, O heavens, and shudder with great horror," declares the LORD.* ⟶*Jeremiah 2:9–12*

Have you realized what has happened to Christians around the world? The only group called to serve God the Father has casually exchanged Him for food and other idols or strongholds. This is not the first time this has happened. Jeremiah tells us that the Israelites exchanged God for worthless idols. So let's listen to this warning, a warning to the religious, to the churchgoers, to God's people—a warning to be careful not to surround yourself with teachings that use the blood of Christ to allow you to exchange gods casually. Jesus' blood was never intended to leave you in Egypt, enslaved to false gods. Jesus was sent to set the captives free by forgiving us of our old loves and showing us the way to love the Father. We get to serve and follow the one true God because of Jesus Christ.

*October 28*

# God, where are You leading me today?

October 29

# Satan's Lies and the False Prophets

*This is what the LORD Almighty says: "Do not listen to what the prophets are prophesying to you; they fill you with false hopes. They speak visions from their own minds, not from the mouth of the LORD. They keep saying to those who despise me, 'The LORD says: You will have peace.' And to all who follow the stubbornness of their hearts they say, 'No harm will come to you.' But which of them has stood in the council of the LORD to see or to hear his word?"* —Jeremiah 23:16–18a

We need to make it a priority to know where our heart is, just like we would want to know where our children are at night. We also need to recognize that Satan is a big fat liar, and that he will always tell us that we are somewhere when we are not. In order to make a dent in this overwhelming delusion brought upon God's people, let's learn about Satan's lies and be aware of false prophets. In other words, Satan is telling us that we are saved from loving the world. Satan tells us, "You are doing fine . . . you don't love the world." False prophets back him up and tell you that you are in God's favor and abiding in Christ, even as your heart continues to sin. If the human heart is so easily deceived, then we of *all* people should be the *most* mindful, careful, watchful, leery, observant, open-eyed, conscientious, and cautious group of people—able to identify exactly the treasures of our hearts, because, like it says in Matthew 6:21, "Where your treasure is, there your heart will be also."

# God, where are You leading me today?

October 31

# The Grass Is Greener in Your Own Yard

*"You adulterous wife! You prefer strangers to your own husband! Every prostitute receives a fee, but you give gifts to all your lovers, bribing them to come to you from everywhere for your illicit favors. So in your prostitution you are the opposite of others; no one runs after you for your favors. You are the very opposite, for you give payment and none is given to you."*
— Ezekiel 16:32–34

God called himself many things to help us understand His intimate love and concern for us. One of the things is "husband-defender." In the book of Hosea, you see the allegory of how we are hurting God by running to other lovers. The above passage from Ezekiel points out that "You (the Israelites) prefer strangers to your own husband (referring to Himself)." What happens in a marriage when one of the partners is looking beyond their vow of love, wanting a look from strangers more than from their own spouse? The "grass is greener on the other side of the fence" syndrome is so false. Once you cross the fence and get close to the grass, it loses that dark green color, and you see what it really is—brown and full of weeds. And when you look back to your own yard, your grass looks greener than it ever did before. Don't believe the lie of Satan. You should have faith that God has given you wonderful, green, healthy grass in your own yard. The spouse God has given you is better than any other spouse out there, and your God is better than any other God. He is the Great I Am. Open your eyes and see what a treasure He is.

*November 1*

# God, where are You leading me today?

November 2

# Should You Be Afraid?

*For rulers hold no terror for those who do right, but for those who do wrong. Do you want to be free from fear of the one in authority? Then do what is right and he will commend you. For he is God's servant to do you good. But if you do wrong, be afraid, for he does not bear the sword for nothing. He is God's servant, an agent of wrath to bring punishment on the wrongdoer. Therefore, it is necessary to submit to the authorities, not only because of possible punishment but also because of conscience.* ━Romans 13:3–5

How many of you know someone at your workplace who always seems to be worried about getting in trouble, even when he feels like he is doing everything he should? Are *you* one of the people who feels this way? This passage from Romans should be very important to you. Think about it—when you do what is right, you do not have to worry about your boss or leader. However, if you do what is wrong, the Bible says to "be afraid." So if you are praying for God's guidance and doing the best you can do, you have no need to be afraid around your boss or supervisor. But search your heart—if you are doing what is wrong or if you are trying to "get away with" as much as you can, then you *do* have reason to be afraid. The Bible says to "be afraid."

# God, where are You leading me today?

_____

_____

_____

_____

_____

_____

_____

_____

_____

_____

_____

_____

_____

_____

_____

_____

_____

_____

_____

_____

_____

_____

_____

_____

_____

_____

*November 4*

# You Are Priceless

*"Are not two sparrows sold for a penny? Yet not one of them will fall to the ground apart from the will of your Father. And even the very hairs of your head are all numbered. So don't be afraid; you are worth more than many sparrows."* —*Matthew 10:29–31*

God feeds and cares for the birds of the air, and He dresses the lilies of the field in splendor. How much more do you think He cares for us, people that He created in His own image? Jesus Himself tells us that we are worth more than many sparrows. Actually, I think it is almost impossible for our limited hearts and minds to comprehend the kind of attention that God gives us each day. He knows how many hairs you have on your head today. He knows things about you that *you* don't even know. How have we let this be taken for granted? How have we missed it? We are all blessed even to be alive, much less to be adored like we are!

*November 5*

# God, where are You leading me today?

_November 6_

# Is Your Heart Lukewarm?

*"I know your deeds, that you are neither cold nor hot. I wish you were either one or the other! So, because you are lukewarm—neither hot nor cold—I am about to spit you out of my mouth. You say, 'I am rich; I have acquired wealth and do not need a thing.' But you do not realize that you are wretched, pitiful, poor, blind and naked."* ——Revelation 3:15–17

*Those whom I love I rebuke and discipline. So be earnest, and repent. Here I am! I stand at the door and knock. If anyone hears my voice and opens the door, I will come in and eat with him, and he with me.* ——Revelation 3:19–20

The torture zone is a condition of the heart where it is neither hot nor cold—it is lukewarm. This was the condition of the church of Laodicea to whom was written the above message. The most torturous place is in the middle of the road, where you don't have strong feelings in any direction. God reveals His feelings about this type of heart: He states that He will spit you out of His mouth! When you are floundering between one state or the other, God is upset with you, and you don't even like yourself. If you find yourself in this position, pray that God will reveal the direction you should go and the attitude you should have. He is knocking at the door of your heart even as you are reading this. Then be strong as you obey His leading, and you will be so happy!

# God, where are You leading me today?

_November 8_

# The Kingdom Belongs to Such as These

*People were bringing little children to Jesus to have him touch them, but the disciples rebuked them. When Jesus saw this, he was indignant. He said to them, "Let the little children come to me, and do not hinder them, for the kingdom of God belongs to such as these."*　　　　*⟶Mark 10:13–14*

We have seen examples of small children, even as young as two years old, who realize that we are supposed to eat only when our stomachs are hungry because that is the way God made us. You know, it is amazing that such truth comes from the mouths of babes. The concept of waiting on God for everything, including food, is such a simple idea and is characteristic of a child's heart. We need to relearn this simple Christian concept, and we can learn it easily just by watching our own young children. At the same time, we should encourage our children to keep that trusting attitude of "let go and let God." As many of us have realized lately, it is much easier to keep the right attitude than it is to relearn it later in life.

*November 9*

# God, where are You leading me today?

November 10

# Only a Day?

*"'Why have we fasted,' they say, 'and you have not seen it? Why have we humbled ourselves, and you have not noticed?' Yet on the day of your fasting, you do as you please . . . . You cannot fast as you do today and expect your voice to be heard on high. Is this the kind of fast I have chosen, only a day for a man to humble himself?"* ⎯Isaiah 58:3a,4b–5a

Only one day of cutting back on the food and eating according to what your body needs is not what God is calling you to do. He is asking you to leave the extra food behind *permanently*. Don't try to get away with only *one day* of eating right. That is not acceptable to God. It is like telling Him you love Him for just one day, instead of giving Him your whole heart. And remember, you cannot fool God. He has heard all the excuses and rationalizations before, and He sees what is really in your heart. He knows your true love. If this sounds hard, just keep in mind that if you remain faithful to God, eventually you will wake up and have no desire for extra food. In fact, you will feel full all the time, and you won't even think about food unless your body calls loudly for it!

*November 11*

# God, where are You leading me today?

November 12

# Everyone Must Submit

*Everyone must submit himself to the governing authorities, for there is no authority except that which God has established. The authorities that exist have been established by God. Consequently, he who rebels against the authority is rebelling against what God has instituted.* —Romans 13:1–2a

Governing authority simply means any person who has authority over you. For a child, that might mean his parents or occasionally an older brother. For a wife, her husband. For a working man, his boss, whether the boss is male or female. Our authorities must submit to their own authorities. Everyone should submit, because God is speaking through the voice of the ruling authority. Submitting is easy when things are going well and when the authority over you has the same priorities and morals that you do. But many times, submission is tough because the desires of the authority go against our own desires. We must remember that this, too, is planned by the Father. Even when the Israelites were taken into captivity by abusive rulers, God allowed that to happen so that the Israelites would ultimately and eventually have the right attitude of submission toward Him. So even if things seem tough or trying, we must submit to our governing authorities or we are directly rebelling against the plan that God has arranged. God will take care of you. Try it.

*November 13*

# God, where are You leading me today?

November 14

# I'd Love to See God on the News

*LORD, I have heard of your fame; I stand in awe of your deeds, O LORD. Renew them in our day, in our time make them known; in wrath remember mercy.* ━━*Habakkuk 3:2*

It really bothers me that God is not in the headline news every night. I would love to hear a newscaster say, "And the hand of God spared this person from a fatal accident."

It makes me mad that God is not on the weather channel every night. Can you imagine hearing the weatherman say, "And God did something new again. We guessed that it was going to rain today, but God decided to bring sunshine instead. What a God of surprises He is! Did anyone see the sunset He painted last night? He outdid Himself again."

Why is God not given credit in all the science books and research? Oh, don't even get me started! My whole soul flares up within me when I get on this subject. Let us all pray, as the prophet Habakkuk did centuries ago, for this arrogant generation. Strive to begin each day standing in awe of God's deeds.

_____

_____

_____

_____

_____

_____

*November 15*

# God, where are You leading me today?

November 16

# You Cannot Camouflage Your Heart

*The only thing that counts is faith expressing itself through love.*
*◆─Galatians 5:6b*

It is true that you cannot do works and get away with disguising the absence of love in your heart. Attempting to camouflage your heart will not get you into His presence. Do you want a marriage partner who does things around you and for you, but who does not genuinely care for you? Of course not! God is no different. Well, what about halfway loving God—is that okay? Should you continue loving your worldly lovers while God is madly in love with you? In other words, should you continue in sin that grace may abound? Romans 6:2 says, "By no means!"

God has gotten down on His knees (so to speak) to propose to you. When you consider that He sacrificed His only Son for your hand in marriage or this covenant relationship, how can you turn this down or run after another lover? This proposal from God demands a response of wholehearted love and faith from us. All throughout the Old and New Testaments, God gets upset at His children for even turning to another lover (idol), much less trying to talk Him into letting all three get into the same bed. That has always been our problem—we want God to let us have our lovers and still be pleased with us. Give it up . . . He never will.

# God, where are You leading me today?

November 18

# You Are Not Far

*"Well said, teacher," the man replied. "You are right in saying that God is one and there is no other but him. To love him with all your heart, with all your understanding and with all your strength, and to love your neighbor as yourself is more important than all burnt offerings and sacrifices." When Jesus saw that he had answered wisely, he said to him, "You are not far from the kingdom of God." And from then on no one dared ask him any more questions.* ━━Mark 12:32–34

Why did Jesus say, "You are not far from the kingdom of heaven?" Couldn't He just have told the man who answered wisely, "You hit the nail on the head; you understand it and you have got it!" Well, it's because just having the *knowledge* of what God is looking for is a beginning, but it is not enough. The journey has to start with the mind, as we discussed before, but it must lead to the *heart*. You can have the knowledge of God and still not have a heart for Him at all. So begin your journey today learning about God's lessons and start loving God with all your heart!

# God, where are You leading me today?

November 20

# Let No Debt Remain

*Give everyone what you owe him: If you owe taxes, pay taxes; if revenue, then revenue; if respect, then respect; if honor, then honor. Let no debt remain outstanding, except the continuing debt to love one another, for he who loves his fellowman has fulfilled the law.* ➤Romans 13:7–8

Jesus tells us in the New Testament that we should love our neighbors as ourselves. This encompasses a lot of things, but one thing it certainly means is that you should give others what is due them. This could mean money, time, attention, respect, acclaim, appreciation, or anything. How have you been treating the people in your family, at church, in your neighborhood, and at work? Who have you shown heartfelt love and concern for today? Pay no mind to how others are treating you, for Jesus was a great example of how we should love others even when we are not shown love by them. Instead, commit your heart to showing love to your fellow man, for by this you will be fulfilling God's law. The only thing we should ever be indebted to is continuing love.

# God, where are You leading me today?

November 22

# Half the Battle Is Over

*How skilled you are at pursuing love! Even the worst of women can learn from your ways.*
                                                              *—Jeremiah 2:33*

You are not a failure. I say this with all my heart. You are not a failure. You've just been applying the wrong procedures to this choice of overindulging or this desire to end the strongholds in your life. You are not lazy . . . in fact, you have been putting a great deal of effort and money into changing your environment (such as the content of food), but it has not worked.

But this is very important—you have what it takes to be thin again or to let go of any stronghold. To change, you must be able to stop loving the world and start loving God. You may feel like you don't have love or that you don't know *how* to love God, but you do. The above passage is referring to the love we have been giving to the world. You *already* have a heart of love, and that is half the battle! It is just that you have been giving your love to strongholds instead of to God. God has seen that you are very skilled at pursuing your true love. For those who love food, He has seen you dream about the food, dress for the food, and care about the content, presentation, taste, and refrigeration of the food. You have listened for the voice of the food and responded when it called your name. You have encouraged others to appreciate the food. Yes, you have been a good advocate for and obedient servant to your food god. So you see, you *are* a good lover—what a relief! Because love is the answer for being set free from strongholds of any kind!

# God, where are You leading me today?

*November 24*

# Put on the New

*You, however, did not come to know Christ that way. Surely you heard of him and were taught in him in accordance with the truth that is in Jesus. You were taught, with regard to your former way of life, to put off your old self, which is being corrupted by its deceitful desires; to be made new in the attitude of your minds; and to put on the new self, created to be like God in true righteousness and holiness. Therefore each of you must put off falsehood and speak truthfully to his neighbor, for we are all members of one body. "In your anger do not sin:" Do not let the sun go down while you are still angry, and do not give the devil a foothold. He who has been stealing must steal no longer, but must work, doing something useful with his own hands, that he may have something to share with those in need.*

*—Ephesians 4:20–28*

Put to death your old habits. God tells us that we must rid ourselves of these things. He does not care how you kill the sinful desires of your old life . . . *just do it.* Do not give your old temptations the time of day. Put out the fire of these desires any way you can. Put the fire out by throwing dust on it, making sure it has no oxygen. This way, you will put to death your old desires and they will not tempt you any more. You will have a new self, following God's desires for your life and your everyday activities!

November 25

# God, where are You leading me today?

November 26

# Give God the Credit He Deserves

*But Moses said, "Here I am among six hundred thousand men on foot, and you say, 'I will give them meat to eat for a whole month!' Would they have enough if flocks and herds were slaughtered for them? Would they have enough if all the fish in the sea were caught for them?"*

*━━Numbers 11:21–22*

God told Moses to tell the people, "Get ready, because I am going to provide meat for everyone tomorrow." Well, even Moses was short-sighted, and he questioned the Lord. We never give God the credit He deserves. Very few people see all of His resources, His power, His coordination, and His genius. God was begging, "Why don't you just trust in me? Why don't you just trust in me?"

*The LORD answered Moses, "Is the LORD's arm too short? You will now see whether or not what I say will come true for you."*  *━━Numbers 11:23*

God has accomplished beyond what I can think or imagine for my own life. He will do the same for you as you continue to pursue righteousness and love. Trust Him!

# God, where are You leading me today?

November 28

# Authority Established by God

*Submit to one another out of reverence for Christ. Wives, submit to your husbands as to the Lord. For the husband is the head of the wife as Christ is the head of the church, his body, of which he is the Savior. Now as the church submits to Christ, so also wives should submit to their husbands in everything. Husbands, love your wives, just as Christ loved the church and gave himself up for her to make her holy, cleansing her by the washing with water through the word, and to present her to himself as a radiant church, without stain or wrinkle or any other blemish, but holy and blameless. In this same way, husbands ought to love their wives as their own bodies. He who loves his wife loves himself.* ⟶*Ephesians 5:21–28*

Don't be afraid to submit to any authority that God has put before you on this earth. Remember, He places all people who are in authority, although we can't understand it sometimes or we know that the authority is less than perfect. When you submit to authority, postponing your own control and relinquishing decisions to God, you are in essence believing in God's timing, waiting for God's permission, blessings, and approval to go ahead. You are proclaiming silently to the world that you believe God is great!

Submission to authority makes everything work smoothly. Have you ever seen people in the workplace who seemed perfectly content under submission—in fact, joyful and almost bubbling with life in that position? They have discovered that submission to authority connects them with the one in authority. The two now have a bridge to get to know one another, which results in becoming interwoven and united, and eventually the employee will be blessed and promoted by the one in authority. It is fun to watch God come back and give you what you want when you submit. You finally see that God speaks through earthly authority. Realizing this makes it easier and easier to submit, until it becomes automatic to trust in God's plan.

## God, where are You leading me today?

# Sin Will Make
# Your Body Ache

*Because of your wrath there is no health in my body; my bones have no soundness because of my sin. My guilt has overwhelmed me like a burden too heavy to bear. My wounds fester and are loathsome because of my sinful folly. I am bowed down and brought very low; all day long I go about mourning. My back is filled with searing pain; there is no health in my body. I am feeble and utterly crushed; I groan in anguish of heart. All my longings lie open before you, O Lord; my sighing is not hidden from you. My heart pounds, my strength fails me; even the light has gone from my eyes. For I am about to fall, and my pain is ever with me. I confess my iniquity; I am troubled by my sin.* ━Psalm 38:3–10,17–18

The physical feeling of guilt and depression is a sick feeling. It is real. You are not imagining it. We can see above that King David experienced guilt and depression in a physical way after his heart went astray. He knows that it is his own sin that has caused his ailments, for he admits, ". . . my bones have no soundness because of my sin." King David is depressed, feeling guilty, and in pain because of his shortcomings in God's eyes. In today's age of overly-prescribed antidepressants, it is important to note that King David does not say that his feelings are the result of a physiological sickness, a chemical misfire, a genetic flaw, or even a dysfunctional family. No, he admits that the source of his sickness is his *own sin*. It is not from an illness to be covered up with medication. It is not from surrounding circumstances. It is from a heart that is in love with or focused on the wrong thing. We should examine our own ailments and depression and confess our iniquities today.

# God, where are You leading me today?

December 2

# Choose Today

*"Now fear the LORD and serve Him with all faithfulness. Throw away the gods your forefathers worshiped beyond the River and in Egypt, and serve the LORD. But if serving the LORD seems undesirable to you, then choose for yourselves this day whom you will serve, whether the gods your forefathers served beyond the River, or the gods of the Amorites, in whose land you are living. But as for me and my household, we will serve the LORD."*
*—Joshua 24:14–15*

What happens if our heart is divided? If we love God, can we love the food, too? Well, my friends, it is simply impossible. Matthew tells us in no uncertain terms that we cannot have two masters. So, you cannot serve both God and food. Now, you were born to love, you were born to worship, and you were born to serve. But you cannot love, worship, and serve two things at one time. It's impossible—even if you want to, you cannot. God ingeniously programmed your heart to work in this way. You must *choose* today which god you will serve: the things of the world or the one true God Almighty.

Practically all the different authors of the Bible brought up this major precept of God. Jesus pointed out that there are two gates—one is wide and leads to destruction, and one is narrow and leads to life. In Joshua 24 above, Joshua makes it clear that there are only two choices—serving other gods or serving the Lord. So be aware, and don't listen to Satan's lie that you can serve two masters. Instead, make your choice to serve our awesome God!

*December 3*

# God, where are You leading me today?

December 4

# Fixing the World by Fixing Your Own Heart

*"Why do you look at the speck of sawdust in your brother's eye and pay no attention to the plank in your own eye? How can you say to your brother, 'Let me take the speck out of your eye,' when all the time there is a plank in your own eye? You hypocrite, first take the plank out of your own eye, and then you will see clearly to remove the speck from your brother's eye."*

*—Matthew 7:3–5*

It is sometimes difficult to tell that the people who love to control are not on the right track. A lot of times, they look the most righteous of all the sinners. After all, they devote their heart and soul to cleaning up the "world." They pour hours of their time and lots of their energy into trying to change everything (and everyone) around them. After cleaning up the home environment and their own family, they work on cleaning up the school and the teachers and curriculum, and then there is the church, and the government . . . . The process is never-ending, but it never leads to looking inward at oneself—after all, they are too busy looking at everyone else! I ask you today to let go of trying to fix anything outside of yourself. Let God take care of all that. Instead, take all that energy and focus on scrubbing down your own heart. It will take all the energy you have—plus the energy of God—to accomplish just that.

# God, where are You leading me today?

_December 6_

# When Willpower Is Long Gone . . .

*So I say, live by the Spirit, and you will not gratify the desires of the sinful nature. For the sinful nature desires what is contrary to the Spirit, and the Spirit what is contrary to the sinful nature. They are in conflict with each other, so that you do not do what you want.* —Galatians 5:16–17

Do you feel tired in the desert? Maybe you are using your own willpower. When you live according to your sinful nature, there is no way you can live the way God desires. These are opposite areas, and you cannot live both ways at once. Our Father wants us to live according to the Spirit, obeying His commands and loving Him above all else. Most of us want to please the Father, but we continually give in to our sinful nature, day after day. Then we pray for forgiveness, try to repent, but again give in when we are tempted by sin the next time.

You see, for most of us, our willpower is long gone. Willpower is our own power that we use to control our actions and thoughts. But you need to realize that true internal control is not willpower, but rather, *God-power*. God-power is so much stronger than our own human willpower. Once you turn to God, you will be drawn to Him and, finding the inner strength to live by the Spirit, you will be surprised to discover that you are repulsed by overindulgence! He makes repulsive what you used to want to do. He makes loving Him your new "want-to." No more battles!

# God, where are You leading me today?

*December 8*

# Moving Your Lips and Not Your Heart

*"Isaiah was right when he prophesied about you hypocrites; as it is written: 'These people honor me with their lips, but their hearts are far from me.'"*
—Mark 7:6

Have you ever heard of the term, "giving lip service?" That means that someone says just what should be said, but their true feelings are just the opposite. They are providing support with their lips by the words they say, but their hearts are far away. Can you verbally give honor and glory to God, and yet your heart not care at all? Of course you can. In fact, your heart could be very far away from the Father right now, even as you read His word and study His lessons. Search your heart, and make sure that you do not repeat history by honoring God only with your lips. Honor Him with your heart, and out of the abundance of the heart, the mouth will speak.

*December 9*

# God, where are You leading me today?

# Perfect Love
# Casts Out Fear

*There is no fear in love. But perfect love drives out fear, because fear has to do with punishment. The one who fears is not made perfect in love.*
*—1 John 4:18*

When you surrender your very life to the Father, you begin to know about His system of justice. You learn to believe in Him as the CEO of all business. You experience how He feeds you, protects you, defends you, and teaches you. You develop trust that He is there for your own good, that He sees your needs, and that He is going to take care of you, just as He has every animal, every bird, every fish of the sea, every baby, every child, every woman and man, every race—*every one*. When we don't know Him, we don't love or trust Him, and our lack of love makes us afraid— afraid that we will not be taken care of. But if you stay in the desert, you can reverse this process. You will learn to love and be loved, and perfect love casts out all fear.

# God, where are You leading me today?

December 12

# Live by the Spirit

*For if you live according to the sinful nature, you will die; but if by the Spirit you put to death the misdeeds of the body, you will live.*
*──Romans 8:13*

The Spirit is not just some vapor or mist. The Spirit of God and Christ is a loving heart and love from above. There is no other source of love. God's Spirit is a "good attitude" spirit. You need to develop the same focus as Christ. What was the mindset or spirit of Christ? It was to please the Father and to do His will. Although just a part of the makeup of the "Spirit" of Christ that is talked about in this passage, that attitude is still an important part. We are talking about the power that raised Christ Jesus from the dead. This power will give life to our mortal bodies! Ask God to take away all the bad spirits and hate within you, and ask for His great personality to fill your heart. He wants you to ask for it, He wants you to have it, and He wants you to live by it. This is a major key to unlocking your strongholds.

*December 13*

# God, where are You leading me today?

*December 14*

# He Sends Lightning with the Rain

*This is what the LORD says: "See, I will stir up the spirit of a destroyer against Babylon and the people of Leb Kamai. I will send foreigners to Babylon to winnow her and to devastate her land . . . "* ━━Jeremiah 51:1–2a

*When He thunders, the waters in the heavens roar; he makes clouds rise from the ends of the earth. He sends lightning with the rain and brings out the wind from his storehouses.* ━━Jeremiah 51:16

*"I will bring them down like lambs to the slaughter, like rams and goats."* ━━Jeremiah 51:40

When will we learn that God is highly involved? From storms and disaster to the best of blessings! After King Nebuchadnezzar lived as an animal in the wild for two years, He lifted his eyes toward heaven and praised God saying, "All the peoples of the earth are regarded as nothing. He does as he pleases with the powers of heaven and the peoples of the earth. No one can hold back his hand or say to him: 'What have you done?'" (Daniel 4:35)

God is God and I love it! I don't want it any other way, and I wouldn't want the world in the hands of anyone else. God has all authority and power, and I respect and uphold every decision He makes.

*December 15*

# God, where are You leading me today?

*December 16*

# Dry Bones

*Then he said to me, "Prophesy to these bones and say to them, 'Dry bones, hear the word of the LORD! This is what the Sovereign LORD says to these bones: I will make breath enter you, and you will come to life. I will attach tendons to you and make flesh come upon you and cover you with skin; I will put breath in you, and you will come to life. Then you will know that I am the LORD.'" Then he said to me: "Son of man, these bones are the whole house of Israel. They say, 'Our bones are dried up and our hope is gone; we are cut off.' Therefore prophesy and say to them: 'This is what the Sovereign LORD says: O my people, I am going to open your graves and bring you up from them; I will bring you back to the land of Israel. Then you, my people, will know that I am the LORD, when I open your graves and bring you up from them. I will put my Spirit in you and you will live, and I will settle you in your own land. Then you will know that I the LORD have spoken, and I have done it, declares the LORD.' "* ━Ezekiel 37:4–6,11–14

If your life seems dry in your desert journey and you just do not have "get-up-and-go" in your bones, then you might just need to call out to the Lord for help. You are nothing without Him, just dry bones with no life. God can put life back in your bones and put His great personality and Spirit back in your heart. This concept is absolutely crucial to life. Death will slowly take over—drying out your very bones—if you do not count on the Lord for everything. Pray for His life inside you today!

*December 17*

# God, where are You leading me today?

December 18

# When You Are Feeling Low

*Praise be to the LORD, for he showed his wonderful love to me when I was in a besieged city. In my alarm I said, "I am cut off from your sight!" Yet you heard my cry for mercy when I called to you for help. Love the LORD, all his saints! The LORD preserves the faithful, but the proud he pays back in full. Be strong and take heart, all you who hope in the LORD.*

*⟶Psalm 31:21–24*

When you are feeling low and cut off from the Lord in the desert of testing, there is only one thing you can do to feel better—drop even lower to your knees. We learn in Psalms that the Lord hears our cries for mercy, and He will hear your cry for help. After a few minutes, you will feel new hope from the Lord, and you will feel like getting back up to face the school of testing that God has created for you. You can almost feel His hand reaching in and helping you to your feet. With your new strength, you might even find yourself singing a song of praise to the Lord!

*December 19*

# God, where are You leading me today?

December 20

# Narrow Is the Road

*"Enter through the narrow gate. For wide is the gate and broad is the road that leads to destruction, and many enter through it. But small is the gate and narrow the road that leads to life, and only a few find it."*

*—Matthew 7:13–14*

Don't be bothered or tempted today because everyone you know rejects the freedom you now have with food. When a person's heart is out of control, it cannot comprehend the freedom that another person could have with regular foods. More than likely you will always be in the minority—but that does not make you wrong. It sometimes means you are exactly right on target! Even though we might be eager to share this way of life with everyone we know, not everyone will understand it. Just as stated above in Matthew, "Narrow is the road that leads to life, and only a few find it."

*December 21*

# God, where are You leading me today?

*December 22*

# You Are Not Worthy

*"Anyone who loves his father or mother more than me is not worthy of me; anyone who loves his son or daughter more than me is not worthy of me; and anyone who does not take his cross and follow me is not worthy of me."*
*—Matthew 10:37–38*

People wrongly say, "I am not worthy of God," because they do not feel good about themselves. Well, Jesus said that you are *precious*. You are *not* worthy if you love something else above Him. Set aside that worn out "I am not worthy" lie.

Now remember, after God tests you with food, He will test you with your family and friends. You must be strong and ready for that test, because God becomes jealous if you love your family members more than you love Him. Making Him first in your life means first above everything, not just first over food or other false idols. Just as we should not make food into a god, we also cannot make our spouse or child into a god. Food has a purpose in our lives, and so do our family members. Pray that God will guide your family according to His will, and pray that He will lead the heart of each family member. And always remember that whatever you give to God, He will give back. In Mark 10:29, Jesus said that no one who has left home or brothers or sisters or mother or father or children or fields for Him and the gospel will fail to receive a hundred times as much in this present age, and in the age to come will receive eternal life. We need never worry about anything in life if we just remember to keep God first above all else. Not only are the hearts that love worthy, they are wonderful to the Father!

# God, where are You leading me today?

_December 24_

# Lower Yourself and You Will Be Lifted Up

*If you have any encouragement from being united with Christ, if any comfort from his love, if any fellowship with the Spirit, if any tenderness and compassion, then make my joy complete by being like-minded, having the same love, being one in spirit and purpose. Do nothing out of selfish ambition or vain conceit, but in humility consider others better than yourselves. Each of you should look not only to your own interests, but also to the interests of others. Your attitude should be the same as that of Christ Jesus: Who, being in very nature God, did not consider equality with God something to be grasped, but made himself nothing, taking the very nature of a servant, being made in human likeness. And being found in appearance as a man, he humbled himself and became obedient to death—even death on a cross! Therefore God exalted him to the highest place and gave him the name that is above every name, that at the name of Jesus every knee should bow, in heaven and on earth and under the earth, and every tongue confess that Jesus Christ is Lord, to the glory of God the Father.* ——*Philippians 2:1–11*

The world is going to tell you today that you deserve something great in life. In fact, taking care of "number one" will be the most logical temptation in life. You will be tempted to remove yourself from the altar, and emptying yourself will not be natural. But if you give in to the temptation, you will miss the incredible work and rescue of the Mighty Warrior and Savior, our God. You will miss it!

However, if you let your Hero—God Almighty—save you, you will have peace and joy, and you will receive honor from those around you. Remember, Jesus did not give in to the temptation to save Himself from the cross and He is now sitting on the right-hand side of God. Jesus

*December 25*

resolutely set out to obey God and face the death He was called to. You must resolutely set out to obey God, as well. If you do not, you will miss out on letting the True Hero save you. Remember that Jesus rose from the *dead*—do not be afraid of death to yourself, for you will rise!

*As the time approached for him to be taken up to heaven, Jesus resolutely set out for Jerusalem.*                                   *—Luke 9:51*

God, where are You leading me today?

_____

_____

_____

_____

_____

_____

_____

_____

_____

_____

_____

_____

_____

_____

_____

_____

_____

_____

*December 26*

# You Have No One to Fear

*The LORD is my light and my salvation—whom shall I fear? The LORD is the stronghold of my life—of whom shall I be afraid? When evil men advance against me to devour my flesh, when my enemies and my foes attack me, they will stumble and fall. Though an army besiege me, my heart will not fear; though war break out against me, even then will I be confident.*
*—Psalm 27:1–3*

We must remember not to panic when Satan is attacking or falsely accusing the servants of the Lord. After all, if God is the stronghold of your life, you have no one to fear. God will defend you, strengthen you, and guide you. Satan will try everything he can to bring your attitude down, to make you doubt yourself and God, and to thwart any good work you are doing for God's kingdom. Sometimes I think I see a little smoke from Satan and I prepare for trouble. But when I examine it closely, God shows me that there is no fire. Every time I think I see an attack coming, I get on my knees and pray for protection. I rise to my feet, confident of the Lord's power, and by the next day or so the threat of the enemy is over. God puts out all the fires of Satan!

*December 27*

# God, where are You leading me today?

December 28

# Press on toward the Goal

*Not that I have already obtained all this, or have already been made perfect, but I press on to take hold of that for which Christ Jesus took hold of me. Brothers, I do not consider myself yet to have taken hold of it. But one thing I do: Forgetting what is behind and straining toward what is ahead, I press on toward the goal to win the prize for which God has called me heavenward in Christ Jesus.* ━━Philippians 3:12–14

Now, when you mess up and you find that the gravity of sin has pulled your face back down into your plate or into the refrigerator or has made you drive your car to the fast food restaurant even though you are not hungry, then you need to refocus. Get down on your knees and pray. Forget what is behind you, look toward what is ahead, and ask God to refocus your mind. Do not wait until Monday morning to refocus—do it now. People who wait are announcing the deep feelings in their heart; they do not want to let go of the food. Why would you wait till tomorrow if you really felt sad and wanted to get it right for God? Take your focus off of your own greedy desires, because they are the opposite of God's. Keep your Bible with you at all times, so the truth about what God wants for your life is always nearby.

*December 29*

# God, where are You leading me today?

# The Promise of Entering

*Therefore, since the promise of entering his rest still stands, let us be careful that none of you be found to have fallen short of it.* ⟶Hebrews 4:1

The grace of God can be summed up as a proposal from God to us, because He wants to be the object of our affection. It is like being invited to join a company with which you have been seeking employment for a long time. It is a wonderful opportunity to have a new boss! If you have ever had a terrible employer and then got a new job under a very loving employer, it is a rush of emotion for you! It is even kind of fun to turn in your two-week notice to let your old, unbearable slave-driver know that you will not be their slave any longer. God has given us the promise of a wonderful, new job—we will be employed as His devoted followers and defenders, and the rewards will be great!

The prodigal son finally came to his senses and saw the grace of God. He saw that just being invited to be a mere slave in the house of God was an incredible opportunity, not to mention being invited back as a true child of God. Do not snub the grace of God and this awesome proposal from Him.

*December 31*

# Index of Readings

# Index of Readings

# Index of Readings

# Index of Readings

# Index of Readings

# Index of Scriptures

# Index of Scriptures

# Index of Scriptures

# EXODUS
## WEIGH DOWN WORKSHOP
### Out of Egypt ®

Imagine hearing a person say that, for the first time in his life, he was able to eat only three-quarters of a burrito and not desire the remains. Imagine groups meeting together once a week and reporting that the volume of their food intake is decreasing, but they feel happier than they have in years. Imagine people bringing in "before" pictures and sharing their weight loss of 100 pounds. Imagine groups of people of all backgrounds and denominations meeting together on one common ground . . . turning to God for strength. In mid-1998, over 23,000 groups were meeting worldwide.

The Weigh Down Workshop is a Bible-based seminar designed to redirect people to distinguish between physical hunger and spiritual hunger, and it frees participants from thinking about food. It teaches people to replace their relationship to food with a relationship to God, and many are experiencing permanent weight loss as a result.

In a series of 12 weekly classes, Weigh Down participants watch videos that demonstrate the way thin eaters think and behave. The host through these videos is Gwen Shamblin, R.D. Using her nutrition background and her strong Christ-centered approach, Gwen developed these materials that direct you to God for help in controlling bingeing and emotional eating. The sessions are casual and instructional in nature. They start with 1 hour videos which include various testimonials ranging from people who have lost 15–180 pounds to people who no longer have episodes of bulimia and anorexia. And all of this occurs without a diet, pills, or fat-gram counting. It is not religion, but it is a give-and-take relationship with God. "God did not put chocolate, sour cream, or blue cheese dressing down on earth to torture us," says Gwen. "Rather, God put them on earth for our enjoyment, and you can learn to eat them with control no matter how 'out of control' you feel!"

After the video, the remaining class time is used for sharing and praying. There are no embarrassing weigh-ins. In contrast, you will hear how people have gone to God for help and have experienced God taking away the desire to eat the second half of a meal. All forms of victory over emotional eating are shared, including weight loss, reduced stress, and a closer relationship with God.

The Weigh Down Workshop presents revolutionary information. Many attempts are made in this day and age to make the environment change—making food lower in fat, taking pills, using liquid fasts, and doing "have-to" exercise routines. This reasonably priced weight-loss seminar is spreading rapidly because the workshop introduces *heart* modification. People are making the choice to love God in place of the refrigerator, resulting in dramatic changes in many areas of people's lives. Perdue Research Group, an independent marketing research firm, reports that 92 percent of the people who go through the Weigh Down Workshop consider it a success. The average weight loss is one pound per week, according to the Perdue study.

If you are interested in a class location near you, all you need to do is call, write, e-mail, or fax the Weigh Down Workshop at:

Weigh Down Workshop
P.O. Box 689099
Franklin, Tennessee 37068-9099
Phone:    (800) 844-5208
Fax:      (800) 340-2142
e-mail:   info@wdworkshop.com
website:  www.wdworkshop.com

An Outreach Director will answer your phone call or letter and help you locate a class near you.